EARLY PRAISE FOR
GOD AND CANCEL CULTURE

Stephen Strang is undoubtedly one of the most influential Christian leaders of our time. It's been a pleasure to watch his success as an author grow over the last few years, knowing he is a trusted source of information people can turn to in difficult times. In his latest book, *God and Cancel Culture*, Stephen boldly confronts the ugly assault that has been unleashed on conservative and Christian voices in our country and offers a fresh perspective of hope and faith for the future. You'll want to read every word!

—Gov. Mike Huckabee
Best-Selling Author; Host, *Huckabee*

When you hear a phrase like "cancel culture," you know it's bad. Why? Stephen Strang, as always, explains in detail. In chapter 1 he mentions Anita Bryant, one of the most wonderful Christian entertainers in America. I personally witnessed her life and career almost ruined by this same wicked, devil-inspired phenomenon. All of it is fear based. Read the book, pray, and resist the devil before it's too late!

—Kenneth Copeland
Host, *Believer's Voice of Victory*

It should come as no surprise that I've often faced cancel culture myself, both as pastor and as adviser to the Trump administration's Faith and Opportunity Initiative. In *God and Cancel Culture*, Stephen Strang does a superb job of urging the church to follow God's call to understand the times and rise in action against the evil forces coming against us today.

—Paula White-Cain
Host, *Paula Today*; Life Coach; Author

This is one of the most important books written this year—and one of the scariest. This will help explain why our nation has moved left and is now aggressively censoring anyone who dares to stand in the way or even asks a question. This is what the modern version of Nazi book burning looks like.

—Doug Wead
New York Times Best-Selling Author

Stephen Strang provides the ammunition for the upcoming battle for the soul of America—*God and Cancel Culture*.

—David Lane
Founder, American Renewal Project

Stephen Strang has given us a wake-up call in his new book, *God and Cancel Culture*. As I read Stephen's conclusion, the prayer of the apostles in Acts chapter 4 came to mind. As the authorities were trying to stop them, the apostles prayed for great boldness in preaching the gospel and asked God for signs and wonders to be done in the name of Jesus. Read this book, get awakened to the threats, and then resolve to continue in the teaching of the apostles. Preach the gospel with boldness, with signs and wonders following.

—Gordon Robertson
President, The Christian Broadcasting Network

For thirty years in the military, I was trained to recognize enemies, both foreign and domestic, that want to harm the American people. Stephen Strang stands as a watchman, sounding the alarm, calling for all to wake up and recognize the reprehensible and immoral activity taking place right now. Read *God and Cancel Culture* so that you will be informed of the dangers looming over all of us. Take action, follow Stephen's recommendations, and get involved.

—Evan J. Trinkle
Colonel, US Army (Ret.)

Stephen Strang's new book pointedly shows us what's at stake if we ignore this trend and how freedom-loving Americans can stand boldly against it. It has my highest recommendation. Get it. Read it. Share it.

—CHRISTOPHER RUDDY
CEO, NEWSMAX MEDIA

Stephen Strang once again honors God's call on his life as a watchman on the wall. He describes the cultural condition of an unhinged society prone to godlessness, lawlessness, and disrespect. But it's not all gloom and doom; there is hope that begins with a revival of one. As much as it could count on any of us, may we stand up to the challenge of these times. And after doing all to stand, we are encouraged to keep standing because the God we serve is for us. Strang's new book, *God and Cancel Culture*, will serve you well in this day-to-day battle. Time to warrior up!

—BILL MARTINEZ
RADIO HOST; CEO, BILL MARTINEZ MEDIA

In *God and Cancel Culture*, Stephen Strang unflinchingly exposes how cancel culture is a tool to muzzle and control Americans. Those on the Left claim to be tolerant, but they refuse to allow dissent. The stakes are high. Let this book help you take courage and act.

—ERIC METAXAS
BEST-SELLING AUTHOR; HOST, *THE ERIC METAXAS SHOW*

Stephen Strang has written an exceptionally well-researched, eye-opening book. It took considerable courage to write its contents. It is, perhaps, a journalist's Christian George Orwell's *Nineteen Eighty-Four*. It contains truths and warnings that every Christian needs to read and prayerfully consider. It will drive you to your knees and awaken your heart to stand for the soul of the nation.

—CINDY JACOBS
COFOUNDER, GENERALS INTERNATIONAL

Cancel culture has gone rogue—ripping and tearing at the heart and soul of America and modern-day Christianity. Something must change, and it is needed now more than ever. Stephen takes a hard dive into this war zone and provides a thought-provoking discussion for the road forward.

—TIM CLINTON
PRESIDENT, AMERICAN ASSOC. OF CHRISTIAN COUNSELORS

Stephen Strang has done a masterful job in outlining what cancel culture is. The book is a must-read if you want to understand the celerity of the advancement of this corrosive agenda in our culture and nation and what it means to Christians. It is time to stand and protect our God-given right to have a voice.

—NICHOLAS LOGAN
FOUNDER, CORNERSTONE PAYMENT SYSTEMS

I have personally experienced cancel culture in my church as Satan used governmental authority to serve me with a cease and desist order at my own home for simply refusing to close our church during the pandemic. God showed Himself faithful to overthrow cancel culture as our county sheriff, Glenn Hamilton, deputized our entire church, exempting us from the governor's health order.

In *God and Cancel Culture*, Stephen takes you on a journey to empower you with the holy boldness needed to counteract cancel culture. Every church leader, conservative business leader, and political leader with conservative values must read this book, which will equip you to clearly see the spiritual warfare of deception that resides in cancel culture.

—CALEB COOPER
PASTOR, NEW HOPE REVIVAL CHURCH

GOD
and
CANCEL CULTURE

STAND STRONG BEFORE IT'S TOO LATE

GOD

and

CANCEL CULTURE

STEPHEN E. STRANG

FRONT
LINE

GOD AND CANCEL CULTURE by Stephen E. Strang
Published by FrontLine
Charisma House
600 Rinehart Road, Lake Mary, Florida 32746

Visit the author's website at charismamag.com, SteveStrangBooks.com.

Cataloging-in-Publication Data is on file with the Library of Congress. International Standard Book Number: 978-1-63641-062-3
E-book ISBN: 978-1-63641-063-0

21 22 23 24 25 — 9 8 7 6 5 4 3 2 1
Printed in the United States of America

Most Charisma House products are available at special quantity discounts for bulk purchase for sales promotions, premiums, fund-raising, and educational needs. For details, call us at (407) 333-0600 or visit our website at www.charismahouse.com.

This book is dedicated to every person who has been canceled on social media platforms, lost a job, had a nasty article written about him or her, or been blasted for the sole offense of saying or believing something that offends the "tolerant" Left—especially to those who stand for Christian principles and the American ideals that made this the land of the free and the home of the brave.

TABLE OF CONTENTS

FOREWORD

by Mike Lindell

IF YOU KNOW anything about me, you know that 2021 has been much more than a pillow fight! By now most people are familiar with my story. For those who aren't, I share it in my book, *What Are the Odds? From Crack Addict to CEO*. Suffice it to say, I've survived a lot of things, including near-death experiences and decades of addiction to crack cocaine. Long before recent events, I'd been rejected and turned away. When I invented MyPillow, every distributor and big-box store turned me down—and that rejection ironically has come full circle!

But by the grace of God, that's not my whole story. On February 18, 2017, I gave my heart to Christ. On January 16, 2009, I was delivered from addiction. In 2004 I dreamed of a concept for a new pillow that would become MyPillow. And in 2015 I dreamed of meeting with Donald Trump, and a month later he announced he was running for president.

Since the day I met Donald Trump in Trump Tower in August of 2016, I've been attacked like never before. But I have news for all the haters, mobs, and trolls: You're not going to bully me. There are things I believe. I have a voice and a platform, and I'm not afraid to use them.

If I've learned anything in the last few years, it's that people want the truth. They want what's real. But the self-appointed cancel culture elites are doing their best to control the narrative and only allow information that fits their agenda. I've been blocked from Twitter, been sued by Dominion Voting Systems, and had retailers pull my products from their shelves. I've spent months moving around to undisclosed locations due to death threats—all because I've taken a stand for truth and I won't back down.

The obstacles thrown at me throughout my life have all prepared me to stand strong in the face of this relentless assault. The battle I'm engaged in is not about politics; neither is it about Republicans versus Democrats. It's about the First Amendment and our right to free speech. The rights afforded to us under the First Amendment cannot be taken for granted, and we must never let them be taken away. This is a battle we cannot back down from—even if it takes everything we have to win it.

That's why I'm so grateful for friends such as Stephen Strang who stand beside me in the fray, equally prepared to fight for our freedoms and unwavering in their faith. I first met Stephen at a Christian media convention called NRB in 2019, and I got to know him better when he interviewed me for an article in *Charisma* magazine in November of 2020 on the heels of one of the most contentious elections in US history. I immediately sensed that Stephen is a comrade in arms, a foxhole buddy who is fighting in the trenches for the same values and beliefs as mine.

I applaud his courage to publish this much-needed book. *God and Cancel Culture* is a crucial wake-up call for Americans as we stand at the most important crossroads in our nation's history. What's at stake is, quite literally, America's future. Stephen unsparingly exposes the bullying tactics liberals are using to intimidate conservatives and Christians into silence—and how believers can stand against them. He correctly recognizes that what the Left wants is not tolerance; it's domination, everyone falling in lockstep with its agenda. And that agenda reeks of communism, whether or not leftists admit it.

If you are a Christian, I pray this book will encourage you to step out in faith and speak the truth. I also pray it gives hope to every patriot who refuses to be silenced and canceled by political correctness police and socialists in sheep's clothing.

Since I first stepped out, I've been attacked daily in the media. My Christian faith and my recovery from addiction have been maligned.

I've become the poster child on the front lines of the vicious culture war, and it has cut across all channels. I've seen cancel culture at its finest, but I'm here to tell you that I remain positive in spite of the difficulties.

In fact, I believe all this has happened for a reason. As people watch what is happening to me, everybody can see what will be taken from all of us if we don't put a stop to it. We need to recognize that and not give in out of fear. Fear keeps us quiet. We think, "I better not say that if it's politically incorrect. I'll be sued," or, "Don't say that, or you'll be attacked like so-and-so." We see what leftists do to cancel people and take them out, and we think, "I don't want that to happen to me." If you've thought that, here's the most important thing for you to understand: *everything you are afraid of losing will all be gone anyway if you don't stand up now and speak your mind.*

This is it. This is the turning point. We are living in the greatest time in history because miracles are about to unfold. If we all stand up and speak our minds, I believe we're going to have the greatest uniting of our country and the greatest revival the church has ever seen. As people come to Jesus, we'll truly be one nation under God.

I see God's hand in everything that is happening. If you don't see it, or if you think God hasn't answered your prayers for our nation and our leaders, then I encourage you to read books like this one that will put things into perspective for you. Though the situation is dire, *God and Cancel Culture* shows us that there is hope. Stephen is realistic but he's not all doom and gloom. Like me, he knows that God is still on the throne.

In addition to reading books like this one, you need to seek God's will, and it's found in His Word, the Bible. As you seek His will in the Word, you can become proactive in prayer. And as you become proactive in prayer, you'll start to put yourself out there in faith, believing that God will be with you to accomplish His will.

Look, we've seen what the devil can do to our country in one short year. Just wait until we see what God can do! Like I told Stephen when he interviewed me for his podcast, I fully believe we're going to look back on all of this someday and say, "Wow, if it hadn't all happened exactly the way it did, we wouldn't have ended up in such a great place." I believe the most amazing days of our country are yet to come. That's why I'm always positive no matter what happens to me. It has never been about me anyway. I give all the glory to God and trust Him for the outcome.

I'm glad you've chosen to read this book. Tell others you know to read it too. Let's rally people across the country to rise up and speak out. Let's join our voices and make ourselves heard, and together we can cancel the cancel culture!

—MIKE LINDELL

INVENTOR, ENTREPRENEUR, ACTIVIST, AND BEST-SELLING AUTHOR

Introduction

TAKING INITIATIVE IN THE FACE OF CANCEL CULTURE

THIS BOOK IS not about Donald Trump. You might have assumed that it was since I've written four books with his name in the title, and you may think this is just one more. Rather this book is about one of the most important, alarming, and life-impacting trends in America today. People call it "cancel culture." What this is, why it is happening, and where it may be taking us speaks profoundly and prophetically about where America is spiritually and culturally—and what the future holds for society, the church, and each of us personally.

To be blunt, there is no avoiding cancel culture. It affects what you see and hear, the news you get, the education your kids (and you) receive, how normal citizens are treated in society, how Christians especially are treated, how we are allowed to run our businesses, our families, our churches, and much more. By its very nature, cancel culture is pervasive—it leaves no stone unturned.

It is no secret that more and more Christians find themselves the targets of social media and corporate powers that delete them, block them, or shadowban them in an effort to undermine their legitimacy and credibility. Questions emerge:

- Who is doing this?
- Why are they doing it?
- Who are the main targets?

1

- How should Christians react to those in power who want to silence them?

- Can "cancellation" be avoided?

- What do leading trustworthy Christian and conservative leaders say about this worrisome trend?

- Where is this all heading, and what can we expect life to be like in the near and distant futures?

- What steps can we take now—as individuals, churches, and communities—to shape the future and stop cancellation from taking over society?

An Age-Old Battle

Cancel culture really isn't new. Censorship, propaganda, and coercion have always been tools of the powerful throughout history, going by different names in each generation and under each new, intolerant regime. The purpose is always to silence opponents and control society by dominance and intimidation. At present, liberal policies are advancing, and a secular culture is aggressively trying to eliminate all conservative thought that doesn't agree with it.

If secularists don't like what you say or what you represent, they shut down your social media accounts, take away your ability to make a living, and tell you that you have no right to your opinion. The message of the "tolerant" Left to Christians and conservatives is simple: "Be quiet and go away." Soon, it may be harsher than that.

This is nothing more than a manifestation of the battle between the kingdom of light and the dominion of darkness, which has been raging since before time began. After a few decades in which America seemed like paradise on earth when compared with other nations, we are now stepping back into the mainstream of history, and this timeless conflict is breaking into the open. The battle has come to us. We have no choice but to fight it.

Since the 2020 election, cancellation has been happening at warp speed. In the first months of a new—illegitimate, in the view of many—administration, a rash of executive orders appeared to be moving the nation closer to socialism and a one-world government. While Donald Trump's administration championed causes important to Christians such as support of Israel, protecting the unborn, and advancing the cause of religious freedom, the new reality in America is that conservatives, including many Christians, are being censored as never before. It almost seems this is the beginning of the end, and the Antichrist will appear at any time.

What is happening? Why? Are we heading toward great revival or great persecution? Will righteousness make a resurgence, or are we indeed in for a dark winter? Where does God fit into all this, and what does Scripture say about how to defend biblical truth in this hostile environment?

These are some of the questions—and solutions—we will examine in this book, with the help of some of the most well-respected, seasoned leaders in America.

A Church Divided

What bothers me as I write this introduction is how divided the church appears regarding any workable answer to many of these questions. Among Christians, pick any cultural or political issue, and I can almost guarantee there is not even the appearance of widespread agreement. It seems we are in an unprecedented season of fragmentation, division, and actual separation on many fronts. Instead of going forward in unity, much of the church seems to be moving backward or simply standing still, waiting for what's next.

Many Christians are stunned and discouraged. They saw Donald Trump as their champion and are wondering what happened—and what happens next. It almost seems as if a depression has settled over many in the body of Christ. People are disappointed, despondent, recriminating, finger-pointing, and publicly arguing over who is right, who is wrong, and what to do next. At this point, nobody seems to agree.

I know Christians who are so fed up (and maybe frightened) that they want to check out and find a nation that is more hospitable to our values and beliefs. The Pilgrims fled England to escape government persecution in 1620, but there is nowhere left for American Christians to go—no undiscovered real estate on the planet to provide refuge for the faithful.

Rather, in our day we live with the opposite possibility that, with a one-world government, there will be nowhere to go if surveillance and artificial intelligence help to enforce total submission. Already, China has cameras with facial recognition and microphones for voice recognition seemingly everywhere. GPS tracks our electronic devices and where we drive. Could it be that with internet-connected and self-driving cars, technology could be taken over by authorities to limit or control our travel? What if currency becomes totally digital? Or what if computer chips are implanted into our brains, like the brain-machine interfaces Elon Musk and his neurotechnology company Neuralink are creating?[1] These are truly alarming science fiction scenarios now in the realm of fact.

So far, no one is implanting computer chips into people's brains or regulating travel through self-driving vehicles. But the growing possibility presents even more reason for us to stand up and sound the alarm before it does. I believe perhaps the greatest danger now is that believers will get discouraged, leave the faith, or become part of the progressive wing of the evangelical community where they compromise the gospel and "go along to get along." Worse yet, believers could retreat.

The church has tried retreat before, and it didn't work. In the 1920s Christians were blamed for Prohibition, which was widely unpopular, and when the Depression hit, Christians were blamed for that too because many supported Herbert Hoover's election. The Scopes Monkey Trial, which became an exercise in our public humiliation in 1925, didn't help. In response, Evangelicals (called "fundamentalists" at that time) retreated in the face of adversity, only reemerging under the name "Evangelicals" under Billy Graham and other leaders three decades later.

Evangelicals also came to prominence in the eighteenth and nineteenth centuries during the First and Second Great Awakenings, but of course, those movements were followed by bloody wars: the American Revolution and the Civil War.

History is nothing if not interesting. But it also matters to the Lord that we respond rightly, with courage and vision.

I wrote this book—and brought these voices together—because I bring to the body of Christ a vantage point more than a viewpoint (though I have that too). God has given me a position as a Christian journalist for four decades to survey trends in the church, and in the six-hundred-million-strong Pentecostal-Charismatic wing of the church, probably the largest and most energetic group of Christians on the earth today (though often politically timid and passive as well). I have access to leaders, a journalist's ear and mind, and a way of reacting to things that has proven over the course of my career to bring out the essence of various topics and provide a clearer, more accurate picture of what's going on. God has used this skill of mine— one of the arguably few I have—to shine light on different people and events in the world.

Retreat is the one thing we must not do. We were born into battle, called to advance on every front. We must take ground in the face of cancel culture. We cannot say, "Woe is us," and opt out or accept defeat. God can never be defeated. We must find ways to remain effective and engaged. Paul wrote that all things work together for those who are "called according to His purpose" (Rom. 8:28). That calling is active. It is purposeful and energetic. Each of us can take initiative and move forward from where we are. The body of Christ is a big, diverse family, and we must choose to cheer each other on rather than become a circular firing squad.

Many believers are advancing and taking ground for the kingdom in a time when the kingdom seems to be retreating. These people know the secret that the kingdom never retreats; it only advances even when it appears to be defeated or weak. That is in large part what this book is about—seeing what wise, well-regarded, and proven Christian leaders are saying about the challenges we are living through, especially in the face of cancel culture, and how to overcome them. This will give you hope and encourage you to do what you can in your own sphere of influence. In other words, it will compel you to take initiative.

What is your front? Where are you called to take your place on the battlefield against cancellation? I hope this book helps to clarify those things in your own life.

Remember William Wilberforce and the Clapham Sect, so beautifully portrayed in the movie *Amazing Grace*?[2] England was steeped in the slave trade; in fact, the British were among the first to bring slavery to our shores.[3] Even though England had a state church, the nation's values were anything but Christian. One of the goals of the Clapham Sect was to restore "manners" to the culture.[4] They must have had some success, for the Victorian era that followed was known for its emphasis on etiquette.

More importantly, Wilberforce almost singlehandedly—against odds we can barely imagine—ended slavery in the British Empire several decades before our own bloody Civil War ended it in the United States. Against staggering odds, Wilberforce and his contemporaries stood up, had faith in God, and saw their country change.[5] Why should we think we won't have to fight for our principles now? In my own lifetime I've seen conservative Christian cohorts arise such as Pat Robertson's Christian Coalition, Jerry Falwell's Moral Majority, and more recently, those who felt we were "taxed enough already" and formed what was called the Tea Party movement.[6]

These were not military movements. They were led by principled people, many with strong Christian values, who changed the course of history in their own time. Like them, we must all find specialized roles we can play in the raging cultural and spiritual battle. We must begin to understand what roles will have the biggest impact *now*—before we lose our freedoms entirely.

This new breed of Christians will have backbone. They won't care if they are politically incorrect and get canceled too. I believe these will be the ones who will help lead the prophesied revival Spirit-filled believers have been longing for. Instead of cancellation, we may very well see multitudes flood the altars, get saved, and turn from sin, leading to a renewal in our culture due to the sheer numbers of transformed lives.

To this end, I want to illuminate the present circumstance as best I can for the purpose of doing good—to bring hope while allowing readers to look critically with me at the various approaches vying for our allegiance and attention. In the course of this survey, we will find reason to affirm the various places where people are fighting on the battlefield and validate the perspectives they bring. I am reminded of the Quakers, who were pacifists, and the Union generals and troops, all warring in their own way for the preservation of the United States and the liberation of slaves. They fought on different— and sometimes opposing—battlefields. But their objective was the same. This can also be said for the scene today.

In the face of cancel culture, the body of Christ needs clarity and unity—and right now it has precious little of both. Wounded armies want hope, focus, and encouragement. I do not intend to throw anyone overboard who is standing for the truth in some positive way. In a war, those running the commissary matter as much as those manning the guns. So it is in the day of cancel culture—we must each wage war from our place of assignment.

I approach this almost like a contemporaneous war chronicle, a series of reports from the front lines, some of which may point to burgeoning shifts that bloom into full-blown movements or trends at a future date. We might here capture an early glimpse of the American restoration in progress. I would be surprised if we didn't.

Featuring interviews with a cross section of leaders, this book documents what is happening in our country, how believers can respond, and why we can look to the future with hope. Even though things are bad, we must understand that circumstances have been this bad or worse in the past, and God always came through. He has plans and purposes we don't understand.

Many of our "opponents" aren't even aware this conversation is happening. It's almost a covert activity. The mainstream secular media does not see what Christians do as relevant or important because it goes counter to the left-wing narrative. They want people to believe they won, conservatives lost, and it's time for everyone to move on. In reality, the country is fairly evenly split politically, and many on the Left may still be won over to our side as they see the gospel in action, experience the love of Jesus, and have their eyes opened to the truth. This could be the church's finest hour.

That's why this is neither the time for religious fatalism nor political inaction. Believers must stand strong and take action. We must pray, we must believe God for a great awakening, and we must realize that He remains sovereign over all. No matter how bad things get in the culture or in government, the Bible is true, and "all things work together for good to those who love God" (Rom. 8:28). That's because we are called according to His purpose, and that purpose never goes in reverse.

Let's see what that looks like right now—on the ground—in the day we are living in, as we advance the kingdom of God, which always overcomes cancellation.

Join the conversation with me.

—STEPHEN E. STRANG
LONGWOOD, FLORIDA
APRIL 30, 2021

Chapter 1

WHEN WILL YOU BE CANCELED?

I NEVER REALLY SAW it coming.

Charisma House, the company I founded, has published more than two thousand books. In the past twenty years, many of those books were sold through Amazon, which has gobbled up the book market like a (very clever) shark in a frenzy. The book you are reading was published by Charisma House, as were books by popular authors such as Jonathan Cahn, Dr. Don Colbert, and over the years everyone from John Hagee to John Bevere.

Then, in 2020, without explanation or warning, Amazon stopped stocking certain Charisma House books for a time and even delisted one.

In 2005 we published a book called *The Agenda* by Rev. Lou Sheldon, which predicted much of what has happened since then to advance the LGBTQ agenda. The book, written at a time when both Hillary Clinton and Barack Obama publicly opposed same-sex marriage, remained for sale on Amazon without controversy for almost twenty years. Then it was suddenly yanked in late 2020 apparently for no reason.

At around the same time, while my book *God, Trump, and the 2020 Election*, which advocated for President Trump's reelection, was not removed, Amazon suddenly stopped ordering the print edition, forcing consumers to buy it from third-party sellers. Amazon did this even though the book had been on the market for months and Amazon had sold thousands of copies. After the election, the company suddenly replenished its supply. (Fortunately, we still see a small number of sales every month.)

The speed and brazenness of Amazon's actions took my breath away. Its tactics not only suppressed parts of our message but also have had a financial impact on our authors and our publishing company. Amazon is by far the largest retailer of books. How well would your business do if you suddenly lost your largest sales venue? No longer were some of our books competing in the free marketplace of ideas. The marketplace now came with a padlock, and some of our titles were no longer allowed to compete.

Doug Wead has had a prestigious career as a political counselor to two American presidents. He is a *New York Times* best-selling author whose most recent book is *Inside Trump's White House: The Real Story of His Presidency*. Wead has strong words for Amazon's delisting of certain Christian and conservative books, calling it "the equivalent of the Nazis burning books."[1]

"When the Nazis burned those books…students from the University of Berlin and other universities came out and burned books that they didn't like," Wead said. "That's what Amazon's doing, because there are books that it doesn't like that it won't sell. Now we're hearing that Donald Trump—the five major publishing companies will not publish his book. They refuse to publish the book. So we can't even hear what the memoirs of a former president of the United States have to say. We can only hear what they say happened and what they say he said, not what he says."

Silenced Quietly

Seeing this trend up close, I noticed an especially alarming aspect of how it works. When Amazon stopped stocking our books, it didn't tell us what it was doing or why. We had to discover it for ourselves. Others have had the same experience. Although it notified us when it canceled Lou Sheldon's book, Amazon often acts in silence, leaving authors and publishers wondering what happened and why. To add to the mystery, Amazon banned several books around the same time it updated its rules on hate speech, but it did not say how the banned books contained what the company deemed hate speech.

For instance, when Amazon canceled conservative scholar Ryan T. Anderson's book *When Harry Became Sally: Responding to the Transgender Moment*, it didn't explain how the book violated its hate speech policy until Republican senators Marco Rubio, Mike Lee, Mike Braun, and Josh Hawley sent a letter demanding answers. Only then did Amazon state that it bans books that present transgender identity as a mental disorder.

Too often Amazon leaves publishers to connect the dots and assume their books are no longer available because the content is now considered hate speech. Facebook, Twitter, and YouTube aren't much different. When they remove a video or post, they don't always acknowledge the censorship or let the accused know what exactly it did "wrong."

The removal of Christian and conservative voices from major platforms happens in silence, often leaving little proof that the book or video was censored. Unless someone saves a screenshot, how do you show that your book used to be on Amazon—or your video on YouTube—but now isn't? In most cases these cancellations occur without any public notice, and frustrated victims are left to suffer alone.

Because businesses rely so much on these big platforms, they now err on the side of extreme caution, having no idea if they might be next. Better to leave well enough alone, they say. In an odd but effective sort of way, the tech giants have scored another victory for the Left.

I have known Doug Wead for more than fifty years and have interviewed him several times on my *Strang Report* podcast. On one podcast I asked him if he is aware of this kind of self-censorship and if he has seen it before.

"Oh, absolutely I see that happening," Wead told me. "I saw that happening in Russia. Russia went through a period of great freedom after the collapse [of Communism in 1990], where everybody openly talked about anything they wanted to talk about. Then, as Putin became much more powerful, on trips to Russia, [I noticed] people were very careful about what they would say about Putin. I'd think, 'Why should they care? Why should a waiter or waitress in a restaurant care if the government hears her saying something, making a joke about Putin?' But you can see that they don't want to fight anybody. They don't want any trouble. They don't trust the idea of free speech. They're not truly free."[2]

The *Epoch Times* is one of the few media that report on cancel culture from a conservative point of view. In early 2021 journalist Petr Svab wrote an in-depth article titled "Communist Tactics to Force Self-Censorship Sweeping America," which points out the dangerous consequences of this trend.

"Due to the psychological mechanisms of self-censorship, a single account blocked, a single video deleted, or a book banned can result in a broad chilling of speech. Important policy debates don't occur, news story ideas aren't pitched to editors, and books aren't accepted for publishing, or written to begin with," he wrote. "In some cases, it appears the censors employ the psychological tricks on purpose, achieving maximum suppression with minimal responsibility. These methods aren't new—in fact, they have long been employed by totalitarian regimes."[3]

He went on to say that ordinary people, just to be safe, won't say or write things that are not even being banned. The *Epoch Times* listed several practices now at play in the United States. The first is "vague rules" such as targeting dissidents for "subverting the state" or "spreading rumors." Almost anything can fall under those designations.

"The method appears to now be in play in contemporary America," the article says, noting a point I made earlier. "Amazon recently updated its policies to ban books that contain 'hate speech,' without explaining what it considers as such. Since Amazon controls more than 80 percent of the book retail market, publishers are left to guess whether a book may get the 'hate speech' label and thus be much less profitable to publish."[4]

The article cited Simon & Schuster, one of the largest American publishers, which recently canceled the publication of a major book written by Sen. Josh Hawley (R-MO) just because the senator publicly questioned the outcome of the 2020 presidential election.[5]

"People pull their punches all the time in everything that they say and do for fear that they're going to be punished in some way," Wead said. "After Alexander Solzhenitsyn's arrest in the Soviet Union in 1974, poet Yevgeny Yevtushenko said, 'The truth is replaced by silence, and silence is a lie.' And that's the real danger we have in being too frightened to speak out. Our silence sometimes has become a lie."[6]

What most—even many on the Left—don't realize is that these tactics have been practiced for decades by the Chinese Communist Party (CCP). As the *Epoch Times* reports, "The CCP has been notorious for constantly changing its policies. Allies of the revolution of yesterday found themselves enemies of the Party today, but could expect to be called upon to cooperate with the Party tomorrow. Hence came the saying, 'Party policy is like the moon, it changes every fifteen days.' People have found themselves in a position of constantly trying to figure out how to be in alignment with what the Party is currently saying and even anticipating what the Party might say next and pre-emptively avoid saying anything that might be deemed problematic in the future."[7]

Joel Kilpatrick is a longtime friend, author, journalist, and humorist who has been profiled in *Time* magazine, *USA Today*, and *Christianity Today* and on NPR. He has worked with our publishing house in various ways for a long time as a freelancer and is quite an astute observer of the culture. A podcast we did early during the pandemic exposed Ventura County, California's draconian health measures and was popular and informative. I asked Joel to define cancel culture from his perspective.

"It's a cute little term for what's been happening for a long time," he said. "Leftists don't want anybody else to challenge their thinking, especially in the public square, because their thinking is so full of holes, and it's so anti-freedom. They don't want to have to defend it. So instead of arguing with you, they want to shut you up preemptively. This defined the Soviet Union; it defines present-day China. There's nothing mysterious or new about this. Cancel culture is just totalitarianism under another name."

Like Wead, Kilpatrick has watched with alarm as people "give up freedoms based on fear, or wanting to fit in, or fear of losing their jobs. That's what's shocking to me is how susceptible to fear people are, and then how ready they are to trade in their freedoms," he said. Also, like Wead, he said the chill in the air "reminds me of Germany in the 1930s," and he counsels people to study the writings and life of German dissident and martyr Dietrich Bonhoeffer. (I'll share more on that later from an exclusive interview I did with *Bonhoeffer* author Eric Metaxas.)

"I think Bonhoeffer is a prophetic voice in our generation," Kilpatrick said, "a gift of God to help us discern and understand what's happening in our day—not so we can go along with it, but so we can fight against it."[8]

If Dr. Seuss Can Be Canceled, No One Is Safe

It isn't just Christians and conservatives in the crosshairs of the book cancelers. Some of the most popular children's books of all time are under the microscope too.

Theodor Seuss Geisel, known as Dr. Seuss, whose beloved books entertained and educated generations of children in the last eighty years, suddenly fell out of favor with the politically correct police. In what can only be described as a virtual book burning, it was announced that six Dr. Seuss books will stop being published for containing "racist and insensitive imagery." To make the censorship even more poignant, this happened on the late author's birthday.[9]

"These books portray people in ways that are hurtful and wrong," Dr. Seuss Enterprises told the Associated Press in a statement. The condemned books included *And to Think That I Saw It on Mulberry Street, If I Ran the Zoo, McElligot's Pool, On Beyond Zebra!, Scrambled Eggs Super!,* and *The Cat's Quizzer.*

I am not saying there are no problems with the images in some of Dr. Seuss' books in the eyes of some. But is banning these books the only way to address the problems? According to Dr. Seuss Enterprises, the answer is yes.

"Ceasing sales of these books is only part of our commitment and our broader plan to ensure Dr. Seuss Enterprises's catalog represents and supports all communities and families," the statement read.[10]

Random House Children's Books, Dr. Seuss' publisher, issued a brief statement saying: "We respect the decision of Dr. Seuss Enterprises (DSE) and the work of the panel that reviewed this content last year, and their recommendation."[11] Never mind that former US president Barack Obama once referred to Dr. Seuss as one of America's most "revered wordsmiths" who "used his incredible talent to instill in his most impressionable readers universal values we all hold dear."[12]

But the *Cat in the Hat* author isn't the only one in hot water. The National Education Association, which founded Read Across America Day in 1998, has limited exposure to certain children's series in the past for alleged racist undertones, AP News reported. Critics have targeted the Curious George books because their premise is a White man bringing home a monkey from Africa, and they have taken aim at Laura Ingalls Wilder's portrayals of Native Americans in her Little House novels.[13]

Is there anything different about the Left canceling beloved children's books and regimes coming to power and destroying the vestiges of the last one? It wasn't long ago that American liberals were beside themselves when Islamic terrorists in the Middle East deliberately destroyed great art in non-Islamic areas they had conquered. Yet now the soothing tones of urbane leftists tell us that de-shelving authors such as Dr. Seuss and Laura Ingalls Wilder is for everyone's good. That they are somehow dangerous. That their ideas should not be thought about or interacted with. If this isn't *Fahrenheit 451*–style societal mind control, I don't know what qualifies.

The censorship extends to every area of the book world, not just the children's aisle. Even liberals careless enough to think for themselves are being banned if what they believe doesn't hew to liberal "must-think." Journalist Abigail Shrier knows this firsthand. In 2020 she released *Irreversible Damage: The Transgender Craze Seducing Our Daughters*, in which she writes about the "sudden, severe spike in transgender identification among adolescent girls."[14]

Reporting that the number of females seeking gender-reassignment surgery quadrupled between 2016 and 2017, Shrier wrote in an op-ed that "a growing number of researchers believe social contagion is at play when clusters of girls suddenly announce, as if as one, that they are boys."

"While gender dysphoria has always been vanishingly rare among females, social contagion has not," Shrier wrote. "These are the same high-anxiety, depressive (mostly white) girls who, in previous decades, fell prey to anorexia and bulimia or multiple personality disorder. Now it's gender dysphoria, sometimes along with some or all of those other conditions. Parents are being presented with the seductive idea of transition as a utopian cure-all."[15]

So teenagers who aren't legally old enough to vote or drink are making unalterable medical decisions to deny their biology. It's a serious issue that is being debated even in the homosexual community. Shrier wrote in a *Wall Street Journal* op-ed:

> Many transgender adults, including some I interviewed for the book, agree that teen girls are undergoing medical transition too fast with too little oversight. Others disagree and have written books. Amid a sea of material unskeptically promoting medical transition for teenage girls, there's one book that investigates this phenomenon and urges caution.[16]

That one book—Shrier's—was quickly met with calls for it to be banned. Target stopped selling the book after a Twitter user alleged the book is harmful. And Amazon refused to let her publisher advertise the book.[17] Grace Lavery, an English professor at the University of California, Berkeley, went so far as to tell her followers to "steal Abigail Shrier's book and burn it on a pyre,"[18] a stunning parallel to Nazi book burnings in the 1930s. Nonetheless others were quick to join her. Chase Strangio, the ACLU's deputy director for what it terms "transgender justice," wrote in a tweet that has since been removed, "Abigail Shrier's book is a dangerous polemic with a goal of making people not trans," then later, "Stopping the circulation of this book and these ideas is 100% a hill I will die on."[19]

For those like me who grew up watching the ACLU posture itself as fighting for all kinds of freedoms—even unhealthy and dangerous ones—this about-face almost makes our heads spin. Since when did free speech and research fall outside the protection of the "civil liberties" in the ACLU's own name? "There have been all sorts of signs from the ACLU...that strongly suggest the emergence of liberal political activism at the expense of traditional civil liberties," journalist Glenn Greenwald wrote. "In sum, the ACLU is being pulled and weighted down by the same censorious trends currently plaguing academia, the corporate world and—most dangerously—news organizations."[20]

How on earth did we get here?

Helicopter CEOs

Maybe it was no surprise that a generation of children whose parents shielded them from all discipline and opposing opinions would grow up to create companies and media sources that tolerate nothing but their own point of view. Helicopter parents have produced helicopter CEOs of social media companies and more who consider it their obligation to protect users and customers from the trauma of contrary opinions.

Your views are not allowed to exist in their world. And now they own the playground and define the terms. To participate fully in the society they envision and are currently creating means agreeing with a set of views that falls within a narrow band spanning left to extreme left. Anything less than heel-clicking allegiance is deemed treasonous to the new order. Fences will be erected, social media accounts will be ejected, and force will be applied in the virtual and actual worlds to ensure that your "dangerous" views don't gain any traction.

In early January 2021 something happened that I believed would never, and could never, happen in this country in my lifetime: tens of thousands of Christians and conservatives were suddenly—stunningly—barred from participating on Twitter, Facebook, YouTube, and other social media platforms.[21]

The Big Tech companies, including Apple, Google, and Amazon, then went one outrageous step further and muscled a conservative social media company—Parler—out of the market and effectively out of existence. (It was reborn later, under new owners, as a compliant, brainwashed child of the new Left.) Why? Because Parler would not abide by these companies' narrow definition of allowed speech.[22]

Parler CEO John Matze told Fox News at the time that the company lost "every vendor from text message services to email providers" on the same day after Google, Apple, and Amazon ended their agreements. "Every vendor we talk to says they won't work with us," Matze said in January, "because if Apple doesn't approve and Google doesn't approve, they won't."[23]

Kilpatrick calls it "virtual segregation."

"It's breathtaking how quickly this has happened, and how quickly what they call Big Tech has coalesced around the same goals and the same agenda," Kilpatrick said. "If this is not a wake-up call, I don't know what is. It's impossible just to plug your ears and drown out what's happening today to Christians, conservatives, churches— anyone standing for basic American freedoms."

The victims of this accelerated deplatforming weren't merely those in corporate boardrooms; they were normal people, respected journalists, researchers, and leaders of various kinds who, only months earlier, fell within the mainstream of American politics. But as with the increasingly rapid cycles of the French Revolution, where yesterday's radicals became today's conservatives—and therefore worthy of death—so the guillotine fell on countless accounts, destroying careers, businesses, communities, movements, friendships—and the concept of free speech in a country of free people.

Wead warns that it could get worse—and that few Americans are prepared for what's next.

"What I think we're not prepared for in America is the fact that we don't know what we don't know," Wead said. "Once censorship begins, people get cocky. The people I interviewed all across the former Soviet Union felt pretty confident that they could read between the lines when the government would issue a statement. They'd laugh and chuckle and kind of [think they] really know what's going on— 'The government's lying to us; here's what really must be happening.'

"They had this sense of confidence that they could figure it all out and that the lies of the government were not as damaging as they were. When they experienced freedom, they learned they had been greatly fooled, that huge sections of history had been wiped out in their educational experience there. There were many things they didn't know. So I think the American people aren't prepared for that. There are going to be things we don't know that we don't know."

Orange Crushed

The first time I saw cancel culture in action in a public way was while I was a young journalist working for the *Sentinel Star* (now the *Orlando Sentinel*) in the 1970s. Anita Bryant was a brand ambassador for the Florida Citrus Commission, an important entity in the state of Florida because citrus is such a huge part of our economy. Bryant was a singer and celebrity who had scored four Top 40 hits in the United States in the late 1950s and early 1960s, including a song called "Paper Roses."

Bryant was also an outspoken evangelical Christian—and an

opponent of what were then called "anti-discrimination ordinances," which were covert ways to begin giving homosexuals special status in civic codes. Bryant traveled around to speak against these ordinances where they popped up, usually in large cities. Miami was one of the first to put such pro-gay legislation in place, but Bryant's campaign led the public to reject and overturn Miami's ordinance by a margin of 69 percent to 31 percent.

That's when the backlash from a small minority began.

Homosexuals and their allies in the media and on the city council organized a boycott against orange juice because Bryant was the citrus spokesperson. Soon I heard that the Florida Citrus Commission had relented and dropped Bryant from its ads, a huge victory for homosexuals because in the 1970s they had no significant national political movement.

But remember, cancellation never stops at political defeat. Rather, it must destroy and completely discredit its enemies. Consider how Wikipedia, which is virtually a leftist mouthpiece, describes Bryant in the first sentence on her page: "Anita Jane Bryant (born March 25, 1940) is an American singer and anti-gay rights activist."[24]

Through the cancel culture lens, everyone must first be evaluated by his or her allegiance to the new morality. The entry continues, "In the 1970s, Bryant became known as an outspoken opponent of gay rights in the U.S. In 1977, she ran the 'Save Our Children' campaign to repeal a local ordinance in Dade County, Florida that prohibited discrimination on the basis of sexual orientation. Her involvement with the campaign was condemned by gay rights activists. They were assisted by many other prominent figures in music, film, and television, and retaliated by boycotting the orange juice that she had promoted. This, as well as her later divorce, damaged her financially....The fallout from Bryant's political activism hurt her business and entertainment career. In February 1977, the Singer Corporation rescinded an offer to sponsor a possible weekly variety show because of the 'extensive national publicity arising from [Bryant's] controversial political activities.'"[25]

See how everything in this article paints her negatively? There is no celebration of a wholesome celebrity doing her best to uphold families and healthy identities. It's all discrediting. Further, Bryant holds the distinction of being one of the first people to be publicly "pied" as a political act, done during a television appearance in Iowa in 1977 as a means of public humiliation in response to her stand for biblical morality. "The gay community continued to regard Bryant's name as synonymous with bigotry and homophobia," Wikipedia helpfully reminds us.[26]

The threats implicit in this Wikipedia version of Bryant's life couldn't be clearer: Dare to speak against the new immoral agenda, and you will be torn down in every way; have your career frozen, your finances drained, and your life painted in the worst light; and be publicly humiliated. I see what happened to her as an early example of what was to come—though at the time, the idea of cancel culture controlling the minds of so many seemed like something out of Cold War fiction.

Wead said the urge to silence dissent is so strong that big media conglomerates such as Viacom-owned CBS, Disney-owned ABC, and other media and tech giants are "willing to offend and crush" evangelical Christians, even though they are fully aware that this group makes up 40 percent of their audiences. This, he said, was perceptible in the 1980s and 1990s and has now come into full force. He points to a personal example that sounds like something out of a George Orwell novel.

Wead's daughter Camille Wead started a YouTube channel and a website called The Blonde Politician, on which, like her father, she gives commentary on politics and culture—only with a sense of humor and the perspective of a millennial. "Today my daughter can produce a YouTube video, and it's not only throttled and shadow-banned, but for the first time in my life, I've seen numbers dial back," Wead told me. "She'll produce a YouTube video, and it'll have eight hundred views within a few hours, and by the next morning, it will have been turned down to three hundred views. Sometimes I'll go on

YouTube to see some prominent news story. It will have a few hundred views; it should have millions of views because it's the hottest news story going around and the hottest video going around. This is part of censorship. The things Christians say and do are going to be censored and diminished, and they could be eventually crushed."

He recalls that in the Soviet Union, it was against the law to own a Christmas tree or listen to the composer Handel. But thankfully, conservative Christians aren't the only ones taking note of the dangers of cancellation. A recent Harvard CAPS/Harris Poll reported in *The Hill* in March 2021 showed two of three Americans believe cancel culture poses a threat to freedom, almost double the number (36 percent) who see no threat.

The poll also found that 80 percent of Republicans, compared with only 48 percent of Democrats, consider cancel culture a threat.

"Americans are showing increased and substantial concern about the growth of cancel culture," said Mark Penn, the director of the Harvard CAPS/Harris Poll survey. He warned that tech companies should beware that the public sees them as "acting out of bias tilted towards the Democrats and voters are calling for new regulations to ensure fairness and openness."[27]

The article said Amazon had a strong image compared with Facebook and Twitter, but that image is eroding with decisions to ban books on its platform. This is fascist behavior by definition— what Wead calls "an American corporate version of Communism." Cancel culture has co-opted nearly all traditional media sources and constitutes a public-private partnership to ban a point of view, which, by the way, voted in great enough numbers to elect Trump to office twice, even if he was denied a second term by the courts and the Congress.

I was trained as a newspaper journalist at what, at the time, was the respected College of Journalism and Communications at the University of Florida. But I'm ashamed of the way the press in this country are sounding more like *Pravda*—supporting the ruling party and the political dogma and canceling anyone who doesn't agree with them.

A Negative Harbinger

Of particular concern to me was the shadowbanning of prophetic voices such as that of Rabbi Jonathan Cahn, author of the blockbuster best seller *The Harbinger II: The Return*, who issued a mind-blowing prophetic message for Joe Biden in 2021. Cahn released his powerful, eye-opening message in a video on January 25, 2021, just days after the (many say illegitimate) inauguration.

But Cahn, like a growing number of conservative Christians, found himself a victim of the recent escalation of cancel culture that leaves those not aligned with the Left shut down on social media, their platforms broken and delegitimized. Although his video reached more than a million viewers within one day of its release, it appears that Google and YouTube both tried to suppress it. Cahn told me the main video was removed from all searches, even those on Cahn's own YouTube page. YouTube also added a line to the top of his page that read: "U.S. elections. Joe Biden is the President of the United States. States certify results after ensuring ballots are properly counted and correcting irregularities and errors. Learn more," even though Cahn's video makes no mention of election fraud.[28]

Similarly, Focus on the Family's *Daily Citizen* publication has been banned by Twitter for "hateful" content. Focus on the Family President Jim Daly said in a statement: "It's simply not true. We did no such thing." What the *Daily Citizen* had done was point to a story about Dr. Rachel Levine, named by Biden as assistant secretary of health at the US Department of Health and Human Services, and include a sentence about her transgender status.[29]

Remember that Rachel was born Richard Levine, married while a student at Tulane, and had two children before divorcing in 2013. According to the *Washington Post*, Levine started seeing a therapist in 2001 and around 2008 began growing his hair out before announcing himself a transgender woman.[30] But we're not supposed to question this unusual personal evolution?

Cahn's astonishing message, however, addresses no such issue as transgenderism. Instead, its biblical, prophetic focus begins with a page from history. "Two hundred and thirty-two years ago in the first-ever presidential inauguration," he said, "the nation's first president addressed a jubilant multitude and a nation that was united in shared values and a common hope in America's future.

"In that first-ever presidential address," Cahn continued, "George Washington gave the newborn nation a prophetic warning. He said this: 'The propitious smiles of heaven cannot be expected on a nation that disregards the eternal rules of order and right that heaven itself has ordained.'

"In other words, if America followed the ways of God, His eternal rules of order and right, the blessings of God would remain upon it," Cahn said. "But if America should ever depart from the ways of God, then His blessings would be removed from the land."

He added that at Biden's inauguration, on January 20, 2021, the nation's capital—named after the first president—had become a military zone. Instead of jubilant crowds, there were twenty-five thousand troops and barbed wire.

"There is no war; there is no overt threat from beyond its borders. Rather, the threat comes from within," Cahn continued. "And so the prophetic warning that was given on that day of that first inauguration: the smiles of heaven are being removed from the land."[31]

Does this sound political? Should a prophetic warning be banned? Only by people who want nothing to do with God and who are the reason Cahn sounded the warning.

Cahn's entire message is printed in appendix A, where he articulates how God's warning came in the form of an attack on this nation on September 11, 2001. He explains how the nation has taken God out of the schools and public life, allowed the murder of unborn children through abortion, and enacted laws that oppose what God's Word teaches.

Then, directing his remarks to Biden, Cahn said:

> The voice of God calls out to you and to all to turn and follow
> Him with all your heart, who gave all His heart and life that
> you might be saved. As for America, the problem is not social
> or economic or cultural or political. The problem is ultimately
> spiritual, and so must be the answer. America has turned away
> from God. And its only hope is that it returns to God. Choose
> true greatness and lead in that return or continue in this depar-
> ture from God to destruction and judgment.[32]

Does Everybody Cancel?

I've heard the criticism that all groups censor and cancel to some
degree. Some Christian groups have been known to shun those considered heretics. Or if someone is disciplined by a church, that person
may become persona non grata. Even at *Charisma*, the magazine I
founded, a few ministries that had high-profile scandals are no longer
covered in print or online. But that only means our company is
picking and choosing what to cover, as we do with any story. We are
not deprograming anyone. Someone else can write about those ministries, or they can report on themselves. But we aren't imposing our
will that certain people are to be banned altogether and enforcing it
with the power of a gigantic corporation.

One of the clearest thinkers in the Christian community is a
Messianic Jewish scholar named Michael Brown, a longtime friend
and the author of many books. He's been attacked for his views many
times, but it doesn't seem to faze him. He recently spoke out about
the dangers of the Left's attempt to snuff out anything that doesn't
agree with its politically correct philosophy, even normal public
debate, which President Dwight Eisenhower called "the breath of life"
in a democracy.[33]

In a thoughtful op-ed we ran on the Charisma News website,
Brown pointed out that as far back as 2012, GLAAD (which originally stood for the Gay and Lesbian Alliance Against Defamation)

launched its so-called Commentator Accountability Project. GLAAD urged mainstream media to keep thirty-six "anti-gay" commentators off the air. Its list included respected Christian leaders such as Chuck Colson, Tony Perkins, and Jim Daly, all blacklisted for no reason other than they publicly espoused views GLAAD deemed dangerous.[34] Since then, the list has expanded considerably.[35]

GLAAD explained that the "Commentator Accountability Project (CAP) aims to put critical information about frequent anti-gay interviewees into the hands of newsrooms, editors, hosts and reporters. Journalists or producers who are on deadline often don't have the time to dig into the histories of a commentator. Audiences need to be aware that when they're not talking to the mainstream media, these voices are comparing LGBT people to Nazi Germany, predicting that equal treatment of LGBT people will lead to the total collapse of society, and even making accusations of satanic influence."[36]

Brown opined: "So, these conservative leaders, presented in the most misleading fashion possible, should be kept off the major networks. Their ideas—actually, our ideas, since I was on that list as well—were too toxic to be entertained. Only the pro-gay side could be presented. In light of that, I suggested that GLAAD really stood for the Gay and Lesbian Alliance Against Disagreement. Dissenting positions must be banned."

Brown went on to point out that the attempt to stifle competing viewpoints has expanded well beyond LGBT circles to include the rise of the campus thought police, as well as Big Tech's attempts to censor and control.

"And now, in the aftermath of the storming of the Capitol, the witch hunt is out in full force," Brown wrote. "If you voted for Donald Trump, you too stormed the Capitol. If you supported his policies, you are, by default, a xenophobic white supremacist. If you preferred Trump to Hillary or Biden, you present a real threat to America, and you must be either purged or reeducated. Your words are dangerous. Your views are dangerous. You yourself are dangerous."

Brown continued:

Back in October 2020, Keith Olbermann opined, "The terrorist Trump must be defeated, must be destroyed, must be devoured at the ballot box. And then he, and his enablers, and his supporters, and his collaborators, and the Mike Lees and the William Barrs and the Sean Hannitys and the Mike Pences and the Rudy Giulianis and the Kyle Rittenhouses and the Amy Coney Barretts must be prosecuted and convicted and removed from our society while we try to rebuild it and rebuild the world that Trump has nearly destroyed by turning it over to a virus. Remember it."

Today, the net is being cast even wider, especially when it comes to shutting down opposing views.

During a recent segment on CNN with Brian Stelter, Alex Stamos, a former Facebook chief security officer, said, "We are going to have to figure out the OANN [One America News Network] and Newsmax problem."

Indeed, he noted, "These companies have freedom of speech, but I'm not sure we need Verizon, AT&T, Comcast, and such bringing them into tens of millions of homes."

And so, Stamos concluded, "We have to turn down the capability of these conservative influencers to reach these huge audiences."

They must be stopped in their tracks. Freedom only goes so far.

So the cat is clearly out of the bag. These rightwing nutjobs, who directly incited the storming of the Capitol, must be starved out if not shut down. And this comes from CNN, the last network in America that can accuse other networks of extreme bias while keeping a straight face. Are you kidding me? (For the record, I wish that all networks, on all sides, would be more circumspect in their reporting and rhetoric, given the tumultuous times in which we live.)

Even someone like Katie Couric, hardly considered a radical leftist, could say to Bill Maher, "And the question is how are we going to really almost deprogram these people who have signed up for the cult of Trump." Note that word carefully: deprogram.[37]

Consider the fact that just months ago, two members of Congress sent a joint letter to twelve cable, satellite, and streaming TV companies "urging them to combat the spread of misinformation and requesting more information about their actions to address misinformation, disinformation, conspiracy theories, and lies spread through channels they host," according to a House press release.[38]

"Experts have noted that the right-wing media ecosystem is 'much more susceptible…to disinformation, lies, and half-truths,'" the letter reads. "Right-wing media outlets, like Newsmax, One America News Network (OANN), and Fox News all aired misinformation about the November 2020 elections."[39]

Ironically this came the same month *Time* magazine released an issue with a story titled "The Secret History of the Shadow Campaign That Saved the 2020 Election," which described the organized campaign that canceled what former president Donald J. Trump's supporters say was his landslide victory. One of the most astonishing items in the *Time* article was the role Christians played in the election fraud. As a joint statement pledging the AFL-CIO's and the US Chamber of Commerce's commitment to what they called "protecting the election" was being finalized, "Christian leaders [read 'progressive Christian leaders'] signaled their interest in joining, further broadening its reach."

> The statement was released on Election Day, under the names of Chamber CEO Thomas Donohue, AFL-CIO president Richard Trumka, and the heads of the National Association of Evangelicals and the National African American Clergy Network. "It is imperative that election officials be given the space and time to count every vote in accordance with applicable laws," it stated. "We call on the media, the candidates and the American people to exercise patience with the process and trust in our system, even if it requires more time than

usual." The groups added, "Although we may not always agree
on desired outcomes up and down the ballot, we are united in
our call for the American democratic process." [40]

I applaud Dr. Brown's decades of candid and gracious courage in
combating the Left's groupthink, and I also believe the evangelical
Left, led by those who signed this letter, is one of the greatest dangers
to our nation. The term *evangelical* dates back to Martin Luther but
came into widespread use to differentiate Bible-believing Christians
from those who are Christian in name only back in the 1920s when
the liberal social gospel was in vogue, mainly among denominations
that formed what would become the National Council of Churches.
Other denominations, such as the Assemblies of God, joined to
form the National Association of Evangelicals (NAE) to differentiate
themselves as standing for biblical truth.[41] Now the NAE has made
a gradual shift to the left, so much so that its members compromise
biblical truth for political correctness.

That kind of shift will take the church not into opportunity but
into oblivion—unless we appreciate what America is and hold on
fiercely to what we have.

Canceling Opportunity

My friend Ken Fish—a great Christian thinker and founder of Orbis
Ministries—asks a good question: If America is so bad, as leftists
claim, why do so many people want to come here?

"We wouldn't have a border crisis right now if it weren't for the
fact that millions of people who live south of the Rio Grande River
look at the United States and say, 'There's more opportunity there, I
will have a better life there, my children can get an education there,'"
Fish said. "People say, 'I'm willing to take a risk to come to America.'
Millions of other immigrants did that in decades and centuries gone
by. They may have come from Eastern Europe and also from Western
Europe. America is a nation of immigrants because America has
always been a land of opportunity. Part of what makes it a place of

opportunity is the fact that we have attempted, albeit imperfectly, to create opportunities for everybody."

Fish points to his own life as a powerful example. His great-great-grandparents immigrated and became American farmers and foundrymen, with little thought of higher education. Their diligence in establishing their family in the United States enabled Fish to attend Princeton University (the first in his family to go beyond high school) and become a successful businessman, then a nationally respected minister.

"To say we want to cancel culture is to say we want to destroy all of that opportunity that has historically drawn tens of millions of people to the United States of America. I don't want to cancel that culture," he said. "Now, let's be clear: There have been problems. There have been mistakes made. There are a lot of things that people could say about the injustices, the violence, the racism that have been endemic at times in parts of American society. But the fact remains that from all over the world, people want to come to this country because, in fact, it's better than everywhere else in the world. And I'm not saying that because I'm trying to defend what is now thrown under the bus as American exceptionalism but because it's true."[42]

Meanwhile, the cancellation continues in some surprising and troubling ways—even involving your pillow.

Chapter 2

CANCEL CULTURE IN THE PUBLIC SQUARE

EVERYBODY—EXCEPT THOSE ON the liberal Left—loves Mike Lindell. He's a happy warrior who stands proudly in the public square with MyPillow, one of the great start-up businesses of our era. He's a fighter, and he claims to have poured large sums of money into proving that the 2020 election was fraudulent, pursuing this case for months afterward. He is an effective salesman of his views because he is sincere and believable and has a great testimony.

But Lindell wasn't always involved in politics. He doesn't hesitate to share his story—told in his book *What Are the Odds? From Crack Addict to CEO* and in my feature article on him in the January/February 2021 issue of *Charisma*. He speaks openly of his longtime crack addiction and the miracles God worked in his life even before he fully surrendered to the Lord. Part of that story is the prophetic word God gave him, while he was still in the depths of his addiction, that one day he would have a platform to bring people to Jesus.

And that's how he sees his political involvement—as a "platform for a great revival" in which "all the roads lead to Jesus."[1] In fact, he had a prophetic dream about standing with Trump in his office before he even met the then presidential candidate in August 2016. From that first meeting, Lindell went on to speak at multiple Trump rallies, receive an award for his company's involvement in fighting COVID-19, and become a relentless pursuer of election integrity.

The question is, Is Lindell doing any good? Does it pay to stand in the public square and fight the war of ideas when the other side controls the public square and can mute or mutate your message at will, using all the levers of power in governments, the media, and major corporations? In other words, is he just one of those who want to shout into an oncoming hurricane, hoping to stop it?

I asked Lindell these questions on a recent *Strang Report* podcast and in a series of personal conversations, and he was very open about his purposes, hopes, and goals. The secular media had long ridiculed him for his strong support of Trump, he said, but as he started investigating potential election fraud, the attacks increased. Lindell and others claim to have examined evidence of massive voting irregularities that tipped the scale toward Biden after it appeared Trump would win. I haven't witnessed what Lindell claims to have seen, but the examples I have heard about are very concerning to me and worth investigating.

The problem was that media and internet companies didn't want Lindell to investigate or discuss what he found. "Every time I put up evidence anywhere, it got taken down…and I got attacked, and none of the outlets would put it out there," he told me with his characteristic passion. "I was in the news every single day: 'Mike Lindell lost his Twitter; Mike Lindell lost his MyPillow Twitter; Mike Lindell is getting attacked; he lost four more vendors today, four more outlets, four more retailers.'…So I was the top of the news in this cancel culture battle. What happened then?…I thought, 'Well, I'm going to make a documentary.' And I made the documentary. It took about six, seven days. I got a group together, flew them into a secret location; we filmed all the evidence.…It's absolute proof; it's the miracle we've all been waiting for."[2]

Absolute Proof, a two-hour documentary film hosted by Lindell himself, carefully and factually outlines—in parallel terms to the *Time* magazine story—the trail of lies and misinformation he says is connected to the 2020 presidential election.

When I wrote my book *God, Trump, and the 2020 Election,* I pointed out that voter fraud and ballot harvesting were two ways Trump could lose the election. I said that for the Trump campaign to overcome Democratic voter fraud, it needed to work with state and federal officials to investigate and prosecute election fraud. If the campaign waited until December 2020, it would be too late. Here we are in 2021, and many conservatives, myself included, believe the election was stolen, both by a wholesale changing of laws and by voting irregularities.

Lindell claims the evidence of voter fraud is overwhelming, but cancel culture doesn't even want his questions to be asked. What should have been treated as a triumph of investigative reporting was immediately placed under the guillotine of censorship. *Absolute Proof* was absolutely canceled by all major media and tech companies, which uniformly ignored it. "It was crickets," Lindell said.

Not only that, but these media outlets and personalities turned on him with force. Late-night talk show host Jimmy Kimmel mocked Lindell's former drug habit, saying perhaps there was something inside Lindell's pillows that makes people go insane and that maybe he was on crack cocaine again.[3] But at least insults had the benefit of alerting people to what Lindell was doing. Ignoring it was a still more powerful weapon.

"What the media did to me on *Absolute Proof* was, 'We're just not going to bring it up. We're not going to talk about it. We're not going to discredit; we're not going to do nothing. We're going to bury it,'" he said.

Lindell posted the documentary on his own website and tried to advertise using Google AdWords, then noticed that the price per click rose from a nickel to a dime to fifty cents to a dollar—as if Google were driving him off its ad service by raising his prices.

"I didn't care how much money I spent; I wanted people to see this movie," he said, and he kept spending to advertise it.

Google then disabled Lindell's AdWords account. Wikipedia took over his page, and Vimeo took it down. His documentary lasted only an hour on (Google-owned) YouTube. Facebook put a big label over it saying it contained nudity or profanity—then banned the video outright. Nevertheless, within a few weeks Lindell estimates that more than 150 million worldwide saw the movie.

He uses no publicist but gives reporters at major newspapers and TV shows his direct phone number so they can call him anytime. He is completely available. But when *Absolute Proof* came out, with all its original research on voting irregularities and disturbing claims, his phone sat silent.

"News outlets were afraid to have me on," Lindell told me, saying many were afraid the maker of the voting machines in question would sue. "I went on Newsmax, and the guy walked off the thing because I was talking about Dominion....Right Side Broadcasting Network—I went on there, and I talked about the vaccine, said one thing, that I wouldn't take it, and they took him off YouTube for two weeks.... They were just trying to attack and to punish me and to get rid of Mike Lindell and MyPillow. There's a terrible evil out there behind this."[4]

A Campaign of Total Destruction

But they went further, and this is where cancel culture takes its next sinister step. It's not enough to make a decision about your own business anymore. To refuse to comply with their wishes means risking exclusion from the business world. Business partnerships vanish. Your contract is canceled without explanation.

"Now, whether you're a Democrat or Republican, you're seeing that this is something we've never seen before," Lindell said. "The first thing they do—think back to Nazi Germany—they canceled out free speech....Then you just cancel out people, even if you don't have your voices. Pretty soon you're listening to just one voice, the voice of this evil media....It's all a narrative, whatever narrative they're pushing."[5]

The cancellation of Lindell and his MyPillow products spread quickly through corporate America, pushed swiftly along by an activist group called Sleeping Giants. Bed Bath & Beyond dropped MyPillow. So did Kohl's and the Kroger grocery chain. On and on it went because "they're scared," Lindell said.[6] They branded his opinion and factual presentation as "election conspiracies" and accused him of calling for "insurrection" at the Capitol on January 6.[7]

Lindell said of the twenty-three major retailers that have canceled MyPillow, including Costco, shopping channels, and Canada's home shopping network Today's Shopping Choice (TSC), "I'm not taking them back. They made their choice. I've told them; I talked to them before this happened. I said, 'These are bots and trolls. These are attack groups that have come out to cancel you out. They're not your real customers anyway....These aren't real people.' And they didn't listen, and they all just piled on out of fear that they were going to get boycotted."

This kind of cancellation only works in part because Lindell's platform and credibility seem to have grown due to the attempt to snuff out his business and his opinion. People found and shared his documentary, which went viral without the benefit of Big Tech, and now Lindell is seen for what he is: that rare corporate leader brave enough to stand up to the leftist mob that demands conformity to its views. The attempted "cancellation" may become a coronation by historians for one of the most courageous businessmen in America in 2020 and beyond.

Meanwhile, Lindell is fighting back. "I've hired investigators," he said to me. "These are the best in the world, and they're going to out who hired the hit jobs....Somebody's behind the cancel culture."[8]

He also has taken the fight to the voting-machine company, basically daring it to sue him, which it finally did. Lindell has brought well-known attorney Alan Dershowitz onto MyPillow's team of lawyers and is countersuing in what he hopes will be "the biggest first amendment lawsuit for cancel culture and freedom of speech ever."[9]

After Lindell was sued, he received a rash of calls from the very journalists who had ignored *Absolute Proof* in the first place. When they asked him for quotes about the lawsuit, Mike shot back a question: Did you even watch the documentary? These major reporters all said they had not. Before giving them interviews, he made them watch the long or the short version. Still, many accused him of trying to drum up business for MyPillow—ignoring the fact that the firm was losing frightened retailers by the week.

Political commentator Doug Wead said this dynamic of American corporations banding together with political parties to crush small businesses transcends politics, parties, or ideologies.

"It's both the Republican and Democrat parties," Wead said. "I experienced it forty years inside the establishment Republican Party working with the Bushes. I could see it at work; the major corporations get the money. The smaller companies and institutions are crushed by regulations that they have to keep. The bigger companies, the monopolies, can afford to keep those regulations, so they don't mind. When a stimulus bill is passed, those big companies are excused from keeping those regulations. But meanwhile, those well-intentioned regulations—maybe they help the environment, maybe they help the disabled—but their purpose and utility for the big corporations is to destroy free enterprise and the competition."

Wead noted that Donald Trump was "releasing these angels of small business by deregulating," inviting dozens of companies to bid on government contracts that used to be the province of only one company, such as Boeing. This "made it more competitive and better for the taxpayer and the government but worse for the big monopoly," he said.

When COVID hit, "Donald Trump's great economy was put on hold, and you'll notice that the monopolies stayed open," Wead said. "Churches were closed, restaurants were closed, small businesses were closed, mom-and-pop shops were closed, but Costco was open, Walmart was open, McDonald's was open. All of the monopolies remained open and functioning and making money—more money than they ever made before."

In other words, business owners such as Lindell were caught in two turbulent crosscurrents that came together in 2020 and after: the sudden control of the economy by way of the stimulus package, which picked economic winners and losers and greatly benefited large corporations, and the mania of leftist leaders and their corporate allies to stop Donald Trump from taking his rightful second term.

The practical effect is that the attempted cancellation of any Lindell-affiliated business may hurt his loyal employees, some of whom told me of how they came out of backgrounds of addiction like Lindell himself.

"My twenty-five hundred employees, they're busy....A lot of employees have stock....If you talked to any one of my employees, they would say that's their career. When you come to MyPillow, you rarely leave because it's such a really good pay, really. So we're like a big family," he said.

At present, Lindell and MyPillow are adding dozens of new products and new avenues of sales. He has already received more hits from cancel culture in his attempt to launch his new social media platform, Frank. But Lindell's heart goes beyond his fights with Big Tech. Talk to him for any amount of time, and he encourages you from the Word of God in his relentlessly positive way.

"Every one of us has a calling," he said. "That's why Proverbs 3:5–6 is my favorite thing in the Bible. 'Trust in the Lord with all your heart; lean not on your own understandings; in all ways acknowledge Him, and He will guide your path.'...I've come from some very bad paths....It takes away all the fear....The times we're in right now is like we're living inside of a big movie....You've seen in one year what the devil can do to our country and people. Well, wait to see what God's going to do with His miracle....What we're in right now, we're going to look back—and I can tell everyone this—you're going to look back someday...and say, 'Wow, if this hadn't all happened just the way it did, we wouldn't have ended up in this great spot we're in, the most amazing spot in history,' which I believe is coming."

Cancel culture, Lindell said, is one of God's ways of showing us how quickly things can change and how necessary it is to be vigilant.

"Just think about fourteen months ago," he told me on one of my *Strang Report* podcasts. "We had everything going great and all these freedoms and everything. Look what fourteen short months can do—we are flipped on our heads….Living in fear of being sued, living in fear of this, political correctness that, 'Don't talk about that'… They do a lot of it through bots and trolls and social media now, or in the mainstream media—just boom, attacking a person and then canceling him out."

He continued: "Other people are going, 'Wow, I don't want to end up like that guy.' Well, I'll tell you what, it's all going to be gone if you don't stand up now….This is the turning point in history. We are living in the greatest time in history, I believe. Why? Because we've seen miracles unfold….You've got to be able to speak your mind, stick with it, and don't give in to fear. If we all do that…we're going to get through this and have the greatest uniting of a country you've ever seen in history. And it's going to be the greatest revival, bringing people back to Jesus. We will once again be one nation under God."

Those are emboldening words from one who not only survived cancellation but is even thriving in the face of it.

"I have all kinds of plans to show to people that are out there," he said. "I became kind of the hub of a wheel, where God's put me in this position…blessed me with this huge platform and notoriety…. We can't give in ever to this, especially the cancel culture."

As for now, tens of millions of people believe what Lindell says far more than they believe what most politicians say on any given issue. While so-called public health experts wither under scrutiny of their data and political (and financial) motivations, people such as Lindell who simply stand on principle and fight for free speech and fair elections build credibility, even—and especially—when attacked.

In this way, cancellation can actually have a boomerang effect, as it did when the religious leaders in Jesus' day formed a conspiracy to accuse His followers of grave robbing. It didn't work, and within a couple of hundred years, Christianity was alive and well, while the Roman Empire was not. It may be fair to say that the leaders of tomorrow—like the great men and women of history—are the ones facing threats of cancellation today.

Lindell's main word of advice for all believers is simple: "You need to fear one thing, and that's fear of the Lord. You cannot live in fear anymore."[10]

Credit Cards as Means of Control

One of the little-known arenas where cancellation can manifest in business is in the hidden world of credit card processing. Whether we like it or not, most commerce today runs on credit cards. And although we may not think much about it, the companies that process those cards have a great deal of power.

Nick Logan of Cornerstone Payment Systems explained to me on a podcast that more and more organizations have fallen prey to deplatforming or delegitimizing, where the transaction company refuses to transfer payments to them if they take a conservative or biblical stance.[11]

"If you just google the name of some of these large payment companies and put in 'ministry,' you're going to see what they're doing," Logan said.

In April 2018 a pro-family group called SaveCalifornia.com reported that because its Campaign for Children and Families was opposing radical sex-change bills in the California Legislature, its credit card processing services were turned off by a "so-called Christian donation processing firm that caved to LGBT demands." According to founder Randy Thomasson, the donation processing for SaveCalifornia.com, which describes itself as "a leading West Coast nonprofit, nonpartisan organization standing strong for moral virtues for the common good," was shut down "because of intolerant LGBT activism that regards biblical love as 'hate.'"[12]

Even the sizable Family Research Council (FRC) had its donation processing turned off just before a big event it led in Washington, Logan said. "The company that canceled them really didn't want to support FRC because of their pro-family stand, which has landed them on the Southern Poverty Law Center's hate watch list," Logan said. "Well, their stand is a biblical stand, and if you take those biblical stands, you're going to get falsely labeled and canceled." The same company that deplatformed FRC proudly provides credit card texting services for the organizations that stand opposed to FRC.

By using these mysterious levers of control, processing companies can deleteriously impact a ministry by cutting off what fuels its vital work. It is akin to cutting off the bullets but not seizing the guns.

Logan acknowledges that the business of credit card transactions is complicated and arcane, but his background allows him to offer a simple explanation: "It basically comes down to two things: authorizing credit cards and settling credit cards," Logan said. "Every cardholder chooses what card comes to the top of their wallet. This decision may be driven by credit available, points to be earned, or simply by a family or personal budget. When the consumer selects to make a donation or a purchase, they may use a Visa, Mastercard; they may use the other major cards that are out there. Once presented, the card is authorized, and companies such as Cornerstone Payment Systems enable the ministries or businesses to accept that card and then settle the associated funds (move the money) directly to the businesses or ministries.

"We're the intermediary that says, 'Your card is good,' or 'Your card is declined,' and [if it's good], we work with our member bank partners to move the money to those businesses or ministries," Logan explained. "This is where the problem is, because many [other credit card processing] companies are not allowing this to happen. And when they stop the funds flow, these very righteous ministries aren't receiving their money."

Businesses and ministries need to review their processing regularly for two reasons: pricing and partnerships, Logan said. A simple search engine inquiry will reveal the agendas banks and credit card processing companies support and the partners they are aligned with. "Not all credit card processing companies are created equal," Logan said.[13]

Tim Wildmon, president of the American Family Association (AFA), said this kind of deplatforming has also happened to his organization. In a press release, Wildmon revealed that the company processing the AFA's credit card donations ceased doing so, without warning, the first week of December 2020. Wildmon said he was convinced the action was taken because "we are a Christian ministry, and we take public stands on moral issues."

"We are pursuing legal redress for this overt religious discrimination, but our attorneys have advised us not to name the offenders publicly at this point so as not to compromise the case," Wildmon said in early 2021. "Rest assured, we will as soon as we can. Right now, however, this has disrupted our donation processing at a critical time of the year. This abrupt cancellation is costing the ministry tens of thousands of dollars each day, and that doesn't include legal fees that we will incur as we fight this discrimination. What we're experiencing today is the most serious attack AFA has faced since its inception over 40 years ago."[14]

AFA found a different credit card processing service, but the company that dropped the nonprofit initially refused to release the personal and credit card information to the new processing company.

So in another under-the-radar way, the cancel culture hindered a ministry from receiving donations at the most critical time of year— all accomplished by a behind-the-scenes business entity that in a free and just country would not apply an antibiblical political test to its client.

Canceling Satire?

Seth Dillon bought the Christian satire site the *Babylon Bee* in 2018 after first being a fan. He liked the way the satire website seemed to be an equal opportunity offender, even if it saw things from a right-of-center viewpoint.

However, he immediately ran into cancel culture when so-called fact-checking sites such as Snopes red-flagged the *Bee* for disseminating false information.

"We've gotten into a couple of situations where if we joke too much about targets [the Left doesn't] like, then they start saying things like, 'Oh, are these people really a satire site? Or are they a misinformation outlet that's just trying to deceive people on purpose?'" Dillon told me.

For example, Snopes fact-checked a humorous, obviously fictional story about how CNN had purchased industrial-size washing machines to spin the news before airing it.

"It was an absurd joke, but we almost got kicked off Facebook for it because we were 'spreading fake news' at a time when Facebook was really cracking down on fake news," Dillon said.

That led to a back-and-forth battle with Snopes in which that self-appointed arbiter of truth repeatedly fact-checked the *Bee*'s stories.

"The fact-checks were always filled with this language implying that we were actually deceiving people on purpose," Dillon said.[15]

Then *USA Today* got in on the game.[16] Shortly after Supreme Court justice Ruth Bader Ginsburg passed away, the *Bee* ran a fictional, satirical piece about how the Ninth Circuit Court had overturned her death.

"It was such a silly concept—how do you overturn someone's death?" Dillon told me. "But *USA Today* fact-checked that one. That was funded by Facebook. They cited fifteen sources to refute that joke."

Like Dillon, I am incredulous that we have arrived at a place in history where jokes are no longer judged by whether they are funny—they are treated as serious news and given ominous-sounding "truth ratings."

Dillon, who has had a speaking engagement canceled because a Twitter mob formed to oppose his visit to a campus, said the Left rates as "false" the jokes they don't like "so they can treat the person who made the joke as if they're a dangerous source of disinformation. That's what's happening with us," he said in a podcast interview. It ultimately points to the effectiveness of satire in piercing through issues and illuminating truth.

"I love a quote by G. K. Chesterton," Dillon told me. "He said that humor can get in under the door while seriousness is still fumbling at the handle. That's a beautiful way of putting it. Humor is disarming. People let their guard down when they are laughing about things, and so it's one of the first things that they go after, saying that they need to stop when it's being effectively used as a tool against them."

Babylon Bee's satire sends jabs in both directions, he said. "There's a lot of self-deprecating humor, and we are willing to laugh at ourselves," he said. "That's the whole point of satire, beyond ridiculing bad ideas and confronting hypocrisy—to get ourselves to not take ourselves so seriously, which is a very big problem in today's world."

On that score, he believes the Left's comedy "is dying right now, in large part because there are so many things that they've put beyond the bounds where you're not allowed to joke about them," he told me. "They are restricting speech so much it's starting to affect even their own comedy."

On the bright side, Dillon and the *Bee* have fought back successfully by drawing media attention to these incidents of attempted censorship and discrediting.

"We've been called a far-right misinformation site by the *New York Times*. They said that we traffic misinformation," he recounted. "Brian Stelter at CNN said that we're a fake satire site, whatever that means.[17] So we bring media attention to this stuff, and mock it, and we'll write satirical pieces about them. The attention it generates usually results in them backing off or correcting what they said."

In fact, Snopes changed its entire fact-checking system as a result of its interaction with the *Bee*. The site no longer rates satirical pieces as "false"; it rates them as "labeled satire."

"We have fought back very successfully just by making a lot of noise about it, making people aware of how ridiculous it is that they are trying to mischaracterize us like this," Dillon said.

I asked him more broadly how Christians can win the war against cancellation.

"If we're going to make a dent in the momentum of cancel culture that's been sweeping us away in this big wave lately, it's going to result, from my perspective, from people really getting a backbone," he said.

"The solution is in enough people seeing boldness and bravery and enough examples where they get emboldened to stand up and fight back against it, and just be vocal about what they believe and why they believe it."

In his view, people need to embrace the risk that by speaking up, they may lose jobs or friends or opportunities.

"The problem is, they can't fire all of us," he continued. "Eventually, when people are standing up in large numbers, [cancel culture] loses its power. They're not going to be able to get people out the door on a one-to-one basis anymore. They are going to have a whole army to contend with."[18]

Public Square Punching Bags

Of course, overtly Christian-affiliated or -owned businesses such as Chick-fil-A and Hobby Lobby have been perennial targets of the Left. I remember when Carl's Jr. was considered a Christian company because of founder Carl Karcher's personal beliefs and pro-life support. Within a few years after Karcher left the hamburger chain, it began producing the raunchiest commercials on the airwaves. Apparently the company was tired of taking hits for its righteous stand. It not only caved to pressure but began leading the way in the opposite direction.

Disappointingly, Chick-fil-A, a favorite fast food chain of Christians and many others, seemed to preemptively align itself with leftist doctrines recently by dropping its support of some charities that stand against sexual perversion. And Bethany Christian Services officially announced its recent plan to embrace every kind of so-called family, meaning the foster care and adoption agency heartily and publicly abandoned a scriptural view of marriage. In this chilling effect of the cancel culture, some companies and nonprofits, private and public, no longer stand behind biblical values. They are not canceled, but they self-censor, remain quiet, and abandon biblical morality so not to draw the wrath of their leftist cultural overlords.

This type of self-censorship—which may be the goal of the threat of cancellation—is even more devastating long term.

"People must realize that censoring themselves, they're only giving more power to the bullies because then you're doing the tyrant's work for him, aren't you?" Dillon told me. "They don't have to do anything at that point if you're silencing yourself."

I also appreciate this perspective, offered recently by the *Epoch Times*:

> Censorship in America is peculiar in its form as it's largely not the doing of the government. It's not even necessarily the result of government pressure, though that now seems to be underway as well. Rather, it's based on actors both in and out of government across the American society aligning with an ideology that's totalitarian at its root. It's unlikely that Americans can rely on somebody pushing against the ideology from the top. In fact, the ideology appears now to be endorsed by a majority of the government.
>
> Yet it may be that government measures wouldn't offer a solution as long as a significant share of the population still subscribes to the ideology or is willing to go along with it. As Judge Learned Hand said in his 1944 speech "The Spirit of Liberty": "Liberty lies in the hearts of men and women; when it dies there, no constitution, no law, no court can even do much to help it."[19]

Chapter 3

CONTROLLING PEOPLE THROUGH COVID-19

E VEN PERSONAL HEALTH is not off-limits to cancel culture. COVID-19 became a political bludgeon even before it led to mass lockdowns. As I wrote in my book *God, Trump, and COVID-19*, in January 2020 President Trump quickly shut down the US borders, announcing on January 31 travel restrictions on those coming from China effective February 2, and then, effective March 13, on those coming from Europe, where the virus was spreading quickly. He declared the outbreak a national emergency on March 13.

These swift moves, which eventually would be applauded by most Americans, drew sharp criticism at the time from Democrats, who condemned "Trump's record of hysteria, xenophobia, and fear-mongering" after he announced the China travel restrictions.[1] Trump said Democrats "loudly criticized and protested"[2] his travel restrictions, and one even "called me a racist" because of the decision.[3]

Hypocritically, and somewhat cynically, leftists then jumped to the other side of the issue and tried instead to use the pandemic—as they try to use everything—as a means to control people. Uncertainty and fear were the foundations of their power.

My Bout With COVID-19

COVID-19 caught up with me in December 2020 when I flew to Phoenix to attend an important conference. The trip was full of long days and little sleep, and I quickly wore down my immune system. A few times in the past when this happened, I came home with the flu, which I figured I picked up on an airplane. This time I came home with COVID-19.

My main symptoms were fatigue, which I at first assumed was jet lag, and a persistent fever. I immediately took the test, learned I had the dreaded disease, and went into quarantine for ten days. My wife banished me to a guest room and office at one end of the house, and as far as I know, I gave the virus to no one.

So how did it feel? My personal experience was very mild. I felt better in three days, though I stayed locked away. The common flu has made me much sicker than COVID-19, so I've had a hard time understanding why people panicked over this virus. Yes, people died, but a close friend born a few days before me died of the common flu in early 2019, and we don't panic over the flu. People die in automobile accidents, but we don't ban driving.

Of course, I am not without sympathy for those who have suffered great loss as a result of complications from the virus (I know only four people personally who died with COVID-19, and each was over eighty years old.) Vulnerable people must be very careful, and those who have symptoms should immediately quarantine until they know they are COVID-free. One of my part-time staff members who had severe symptoms went to lunch with other staff members and gave the virus to several more, a couple of whom ended up in the hospital. I am grateful everyone recovered.

Long before I got the disease I was writing and podcasting about this new virus from China. When COVID-19 was first declared a worldwide pandemic, we didn't know how serious it would be. Like many people, I wondered if it would be like the bubonic plague (or Black Death) in Europe in 1347–1353, which killed twenty million to forty million people, or as much as nearly two-thirds of the population. In 2020 I recorded podcasts on the virus in early February, before COVID-19 had hit most people's radar screens. Some were just trying to figure out what was going on. In the February podcast, we examined sources in China who were saying the Chinese Communist government was lying about it.[4] In my biggest podcast ever, in March

2020, I talked about what different Christian leaders were saying about the pandemic.[5] Obviously, interest on the subject was high.

When the lockdown began, our company, Charisma Media, never closed; we were considered "essential" as media. But we had about 75 percent of the staff work from home just to be safe. We practiced social distancing and disinfected everything, and only one of my staff members came down with the virus (which he picked up from a family member) until December, when I tested positive.

But within a few short months from the beginning of the outbreak, the Left had developed a "correct" COVID-19 narrative and begun bullying people into proclaiming their view on vaccines, lockdowns, proper treatments, and such. Seeing that Democrats were not letting this crisis go to waste, and that many states were far more restrictive than the one I lived in, I realized the response to the pandemic would greatly affect the election. I took twenty-one days in April 2020 to write *God, Trump, and COVID-19*, which we released as an e-book and then in print when stores started opening again. By then the politically correct narrative was hardening into place, and those who questioned it were painted as insensitive, anti-science quacks and extremists.

One physician friend of mine experienced the Left's wrath in a highly visible way, both personally and professionally.

Frontline Persecution

Dr. Stella Immanuel's rise to national acclaim—and scorn—began with a hitherto obscure (to non-medical folks such as me) and rather common drug called hydroxychloroquine. The first time I heard of this drug was when President Donald Trump began talking about it, predictably causing the Left to respond with wild rumors and claims of its unproven status. I did my own investigating and found it could be taken as a prophylactic, so I started taking regular doses. I later learned I was taking only half the recommended dosage of both hydroxychloroquine and zinc, which I already took as part of my vitamin regimen. I thought I was immune and was shocked when I tested positive for COVID-19.

But before then, people were buzzing about a group known as America's Frontline Doctors. I watched some of its videos and was impressed with what I heard. It made sense to me that a drug designed to address one concern is often found to be an effective treatment for another. My own doctor had explained this fact concerning a prescription I took at one time. I also heard that one of the Frontline doctors, Dr. Stella Immanuel of Houston, was a Spirit-filled Christian.

That's the audience Charisma Media serves, and we were able to track her down so I could interview her for a podcast. Charisma News called Immanuel a "COVID-busting warrior physician," a great way to describe this Cameroon native who burst onto the national scene for touting a simple and seemingly noncontroversial treatment for the virus.[6]

Early in the pandemic, Immanuel heard from a fellow physician about the use of hydroxychloroquine in treating COVID-19. At Rehoboth Medical Center, the clinic she owns in Houston, "We started using it, and the results were dramatic," she told me. "Where patients came in with COVID symptoms, if they came within the first two, three days, the results were so dramatic that it got better in twenty-four to forty-eight hours. So we started using [hydroxychloroquine] and then [treating them] with zinc and then with vitamin C and [azithromycin]."

Immanuel did more research and found an article from several years earlier that showed "hydroxychloroquine was a potent inhibitor of SARS-COVID," she said. "Because COVID is a group of viruses... they actually act the same way. So it made sense that if it inhibited viral replication, it stopped viral uptake; it opened the zinc channels so that zinc could get into the cell. It only made sense....And of course, we started using it and it worked. It was amazing."

Immanuel treated hundreds of patients, and "everybody's alive. I mean, we treat them, and they get well," she said. Unlike many other COVID-19 patients whose symptoms come and go, her patients "don't get waxing and waning symptoms. They get well....It clears the virus out of their system. It clears the symptoms out of the system. And that is why I call it a cure....People get all crazy: 'You cannot say it's a cure; there's no cure for COVID.' I maintain that there is a cure for COVID. It is hydroxychloroquine; it is zinc and [azithromycin]. I do not understand why they want Americans to die when it's an effective treatment for COVID."[7]

She was referring to the vociferous pushback she and the other Frontline doctors received when they met together in Washington, DC, to educate the public about effective treatments for COVID. The group, led by Dr. Simone Gold, made a video that not only garnered millions of views in a short period of time—Breitbart's video of its press conference accumulated over seventeen million views during the eight hours it was hosted on Facebook[8]—but also exemplified the lengths to which the Left would go to maintain control, not just of cultural narratives but of medical cures.

Gold later told Tucker Carlson she and her fellow physicians "came to Washington because we're so distressed. Frontline doctors like myself, we're seeing patients not get what they need. We're seeing the doctor-patient relationship being completely eroded, that the governors are empowering pharmacies to overrule doctors who had conversations with their patients. It's really something that America should be alarmed about."

Gold pointed out that although that video of the press conference in front of the Supreme Court "got the most attention," the Frontline event itself was "seven hours of doctors teaching the American people.... We went through everything: the lockdown, masks, hydroxychloroquine treatment, other treatments...how it affects older people, younger people, etc. That was actually the majority of the summit."[9]

In a second video, Immanuel stood with a group of several others, most of whom also wore white lab coats, and said, "If they put everybody on hydroxychloroquine right now, for those with early disease... and those that want to get prevention, I'm telling you, it will stop COVID in its tracks in 30 days."[10]

She challenged those who didn't believe her to "look me up....
Look every one of us up. We're physicians. You can find us. We're not
hiding. We're right here."[11]

In the viral video, Gold said, "This is a treatment regimen that's
very simple, and it should be in the hands of the American people.
The difficult aspect of this is that at the moment, because of politics,
it's being blocked from doctors prescribing it, and it's being blocked
from pharmacists releasing it....I'm in favor of it being over-the-
counter. Give it to the people."[12]

"I don't want anyone to just believe me because I'm saying it," Gold
told Tucker Carlson. "We put together a white paper that has all the
science; it's utterly irrefutable that hydroxychloroquine is safe. That's
without question....You have to kind of wonder why we're still talking
about an FDA-approved medication."[13]

Still, Facebook, YouTube, and other Big Tech outlets "were taking
the video down as fast as people were putting it back up," Immanuel
told me later.

Some of the reactions seem to have been politically motivated.
President Trump said on May 18, 2020: "I'm taking it, hydroxychloroquine. Right now, yeah, a couple of weeks ago I started taking it,
because I think it's good. I've heard a lot of good stories."[14] But when
his son Donald Trump Jr. tweeted the Frontline doctors' video, his
Twitter account was restricted for sharing "content that may pose a
risk to people's health."[15] All videos of America's Frontline Doctors
were then stripped from Facebook and YouTube, and the organization's website was taken down.

An avalanche of negative news stories began. These experienced,
licensed physicians were called "quacks" and said to be funded by
"dark money."[16] *USA Today* reported the doctors "don't know what
they're talking about."[17]

"Then came the attacks, the backlash, and people started [saying],
'No, the drug doesn't work,'" Immanuel said. "At some point, it was
even hard to convince our patients to take the medication, because all
[the officials] said was, 'This medication is dangerous. It can kill you.

It can stop your heart.' I said, 'No, this is a safe medication. It's been around for sixty to seventy years. It's very safe.'"[18]

Unbowed by the assault from the cancel culture, Immanuel posted to her Twitter account: "Big Tech is censoring Experts and suppressing the CURE. I will not be silenced."[19]

Gold too was adamant: "You know, I thought I lived in America. You had a bunch of doctors talking literally about science, getting deplatformed. It's outrageous."[20]

Immanuel pointed out something interesting: while the Left tried to silence all the Frontline doctors, it reserved its most vicious attacks for her.

"We realized that this was really not about medicine, that there was something really sinister going on," she told me. "The battle was not a medical battle....It was a propaganda battle; it was a spiritual battle."

The attacks against Immanuel were especially barbed, and she is convinced the furor came because of her status as a Spirit-filled believer.

"I'm a woman of God. I'm a prayer warrior. I'm a deliverance minister; my calling is prophetic," she told me. "For me, it was very spiritual....[I'd been] praying for the nation....There was anointing from the Holy Spirit that came on that day when I spoke, [and] I broke something in the spirit."

She said, "The whole world was catching fear....That day was like a watershed moment, and the Lord just really used my voice to break the spirit of fear over the nations."

Mincing no words, she added, "I believe this was actually the devil. I know he works through people, but he was like, 'Stop her; cancel her; shut her up.'"

As a Charismatic Christian, I know what it's like to be attacked for believing the Bible literally. There are things secular observers don't understand or don't want to understand. Many Christians around the world know what it's like to have some theologians reject their doctrines. But since when do we measure respected physicians by their theology? Every religion has beliefs that can be (and sometimes are) mocked by other religions. I don't agree with Hindu or Mormon beliefs (to name just two), but that doesn't mean I wouldn't allow myself to be treated in an emergency room by a doctor whose understanding of spirituality does not align with mine.

"Diabolical" Motivations

Immanuel's first exposure to drugs in the same class as hydroxychloroquine had nothing to do with the pandemic. She attended medical school in Nigeria and has thus treated many malaria patients with the "-quine" drugs.

"We grew up taking this medicine," she said. "I've been in the US for thirty years now. Even when I travel back home, we take these medicines to prevent malaria, and we give them to other people who are traveling back home."

She adds that many people with conditions such as lupus or rheumatoid arthritis "take this medication daily for years."

Why didn't COVID-19 spread through Nigeria as it did in the United States? As of May 10, 2020, the World Health Organization reported 165,419 cases in Nigeria, or only 0.08 percent of the population, and more than 32.3 million cases in the United States, or 9.8 percent of the population.[21] Immanuel believes it's because when people travel to sub-Saharan countries, they are advised to take antimalarial drugs. Residents of these nations commonly receive the -quine drugs for antimalarial use as well.

Those antimalarials are "very potent against COVID," she said. "So those COVIDs were killed in their system before they could spread through the country. If you notice, most countries that are malaria-endemic that are taking those -quines, their COVID deaths are not that high."[22]

The fight against hydroxychloroquine, Immanuel said, "was an orchestrated thing" ultimately intended to "promote the vaccine agenda."

"Democrats are just opportunistic on this," she said. "But this is way deeper than even Democrats, and most of them don't realize it. That's why I tell Americans, 'Don't let our political factions and our political division allow these diabolic, sinister people to kill us.'…The main issue is there are people who want to make money and want to destroy people, that want to control population, and that is the diabolical part behind this thing."[23]

The Left's obsession with destroying Donald Trump took precedence over keeping Americans healthy and protecting their freedom to control their own health choices, in my view.

Joseph Mercola is another respected doctor who has run afoul with the Left. His website, Mercola.com, is touted as "the #1 natural health website," and it is certainly popular at our house.[24] On his site Mercola offers a perspective of Big Tech's role during the pandemic that I hadn't heard before. The author of *The Truth About COVID-19: Exposing the Great Reset, Lockdowns, Vaccine Passports, and the New Normal*, Mercola believes Big Tech is guilty of cleverly manipulating the population with sophisticated propaganda derived from "decades of data stolen from you and the rest of the population by Google.

"If you rely only on these mainstream media, you will only hear the official propaganda narrative about the pandemic, because everything else has been censored—everything, 100%," he wrote on his website, calling it "a very dark agenda." According to Mercola: "One of the biggest motivating catalysts behind this engineered pandemic is this transfer of wealth from most everyone to a global tyranny. In the long term, the goal is to convert [the population] into digital assets that can be controlled and manipulated. It appears their intent is to put us in a virtual world that essentially makes us digital assets that can be traded. Decentralized options are the solution, which is why we need to develop decentralized censorship-resistant internet and social media platforms."[25]

And so the cancellation rolls on.

Gold, the Los Angeles–based physician and leader of the Frontliners, lost her job because of her advocacy of hydroxychloroquine. Already blocked or removed by most social media outlets, she told Fox News'

Tucker Carlson that she was "summarily fired." Despite her more than twenty years' experience in the medical field, she said her hospital employer let her go for what it termed the "embarrassing video."[26]

"I'm a board-certified emergency room physician," Gold said. "We are pretty hard to come by, and suddenly they don't need me. I mean, it's ridiculous. This is a complete loss of our free speech."[27]

Gold created a brand-new website to host the video of the summit and invited people to visit americasfrontlinedoctorssummit.com to watch it in full.

Immanuel too is still largely blocked from voicing her professional opinions. "Today…if you do a show on YouTube or on Facebook and you advertise that you're going to have me on your show, they're going to send a warning that if you say anything, they're going to take you down," she told me. She regularly experiences this type of censorship, she said.

"The reason they are shutting us down is because they want to put a barrier between the masses hearing the information everybody needs to be safe," Immanuel told me. "This is not just happening in America. It's happening all over the nations of the world. People are calling me from everywhere.…Governments are shutting it down, not just here, but all over. So there's been a medical cancel culture going [on] all over the world."

The effort to silence her and others has definitely "hindered my voice or the level that my voice could have reached," she told me, primarily "because a lot of people who would have talked to me got scared that if they talked to me or if they published me…"

In other words, they self-censored. But Immanuel remains uncowed.

"[I] have no fear because I'm a child of God," she told me. "I have a bold voice. Most other people, they filter what they say in the cancel culture filter. I don't."

She and some partners have started a prayer program to engage in "prayer warfare, fighting for the nation," she told me.

"The church is the only entity that has been given the mandate to fight this evil," she said. "But the church has been shut down, and the church is weak, and the church is asleep. So the warriors that are supposed to get up and stop this are actually out there in the valley of dry bones. So part of our duty right now is to prayer and calling for God to wake up the remnants and bring them out of [the] valley of dry bones so we can fight this battle....[We] need to wake up and pray...that the veil that's upon the minds of people will be gone. The leaders in the church, those that are still real leaders in the church, need to start calling for mass prayer rallies. They need to start calling for people to rise up and pray, rise up and repent before God."

Immanuel then seemed to catch a prophetic flow, addressing the church from the mountaintop of her medical profession.

"Where are the prophetic voices in the church?" she asked. "Where are the leaders in the church to rise up and say, 'No, stop'? These are supposed to be the people that are discipling the world. The church that's supposed to be the voice of hope has cowered down, accepted the cancel culture, and sat down....Our commission was, 'Go into the world; make disciples of nations.' The nations are going to hell right now because the church refused to disciple the nations. We stayed in our...churches, claimed our breakthrough, our next level, followed our own assumptions...[but] we've left the work....This whole thing that is happening in our generation is a fault of the church, because we were the people who were supposed to keep the world safe."

Still, she has a bright outlook on the future.

"God is still able to redeem," this Frontline warrior told me. In some ways, her voice has greater reach and credibility than ever because of the attempted cancellation. And certainly her ministry has gone from a medical practice in Houston to now impacting the whole world.

Immanuel hasn't backed down—and neither should we.

Chapter 4

HOW THE CULTURE IS CANCELING CHRISTIANITY

O NE OF MY longtime friends leads a respected national ministry, and his wife is a real estate agent in their city. The
company his wife founded shares office space with the
ministry my friend leads, and both the business and the ministry
have been thriving together for years.

But in late 2020, my friend's wife received a startling letter from
the National Association of Realtors, a collective organization for all
real estate agents licensed in their respective states. It announced that
the organization had revised its code of ethics to prohibit Realtors
from using "harassing speech, hate speech, epithets, or slurs based
on race, color, religion, sex, handicap, familial status, national origin,
sexual orientation, or gender identity." Member agents must comply
with the ethics code in "all of their activities," and those who violate
it are subject to disciplinary action.[1]

According to my friends, though the ethics code is couched in the
language of anti-discrimination, the revised policy means that if a
Realtor posts a Bible verse on his or her personal Facebook page and
someone in the sexual orientation or gender identity protected classes
is offended, that post could be deemed hate speech and that Realtor
could face disciplinary action, ranging from a fine to the loss of his
or her license.

"My wife read this and said, 'Thousands of believers who are real
estate agents will be out of business,'" my friend told me. His wife's
heart went out to those agents in mid-career, with families and homes,

who would be thrown into either moral or financial crisis by the sudden move.

"This alerted her because she's watching the things increase in the culture, and she's really levelheaded and says, 'We'll be fine.' But she read that and goes, 'I am now officially not OK. I am troubled at a whole other level,'" my friend related to me. "She said, 'I'm thinking of the people I know, not just my own life. I know Realtors; we're strong friends, even in other companies across the city. I know their kids; they love the Lord. They are going to lose their job based on this.'"

In my friend's view, this is a preview of coming attractions as the exclusion of Christians and others who hold to biblical morality is multiplied in profession after profession. This will be especially true if extreme legislation such as the nice-sounding Equality Act, which redefines gender completely, passes. (In mid-2021, when I wrote this, it had passed the US House but not the US Senate.)

"The Equality Act will be the most devastating promotion of litigation and laws to stop religious liberty," my friend warned, citing this piece of legislation supported by the Biden administration. This bill expands the 1964 Civil Rights Act by broadening the definition of *protected classes* to include gender identity and sexual orientation. "It will stop people who value the Bible from walking out our conscience, being inspired and loyal to the Bible," my friend said. "It will snuff out other religious groups as well—synagogues and mosques and all kinds of different religious gatherings. Evangelical Christians who believe the Bible will be absolutely slammed by this....This is terrifying in its implications."[2]

The Sacred Ceiling

I would like to think such legislation has no chance of passing, but reality says otherwise. One hundred percent of Democrats in the House of Representatives voted for it, and their mindset is that this is inevitable and "good." If Christians are discriminated against as a result, the Democrats' response is essentially, "They deserve it!" Taken to its logical conclusion, it means that eventually the Bible will be outlawed as a hate book.

For now, many people fall into the same category as my friend's wife, the real estate agent. They've been hoping Christians would be able to ride out the storm but are increasingly facing a rude reality: cancel culture eventually hits everyone.

I suppose that realization struck me early in my journalism career. It was the 1970s, but I was very aware that the people in the newsroom, who knew I was an evangelical Christian, treated me like an outsider. The accepted belief system in the newsroom was secular humanism. I figured out quickly that I had no upward mobility, which is one reason I left the secular journalism profession. I don't remember the people being unkind necessarily, but I was excluded from certain assignments and marginalized. Some of the editors were passionate for their secular worldview almost as if it were a religion. I was aware they kept an eye on me to be sure I didn't sneak something about God into an article.[3]

For me, the understanding came intuitively that there was disdain for my evangelical beliefs. Nowadays the discrimination—as the example of my friend's wife shows—is overt and far-reaching. I'm not sure there is any professional arena in America where Christians are free to speak about (let alone promote) the biblical perspective on all types of morality. How can you serve as a public-school teacher in California while not compromising your Christian beliefs regarding marriage and families? The same could be asked about the counseling profession, the legal profession, or higher education.

Ken Fish of Orbis Ministries said cancel culture is specifically an attack on the Bible.

"When we talk about cancel culture, we're not just dealing with… capitalism…we are actually talking about destroying Christianity," he told me, and he pointed out that during the riots of 2020, some of the people gathered in Portland used Bibles to start a bonfire.[4] Isn't this a step toward the way Hitler burned books in the 1930s, just before the Second World War? Who would have thought this would ever happen in America?

And yet from society came a collective yawn. Sure, leaders such as Ted Cruz and Donald Trump Jr. tweeted about the incident, and there were some news reports about it, especially in conservative media. But most people just shrugged and went back to work or play. One of the more deeply disturbing things to me about all that happened in 2020 and beyond is how passively the population, including patriots and Christians, responded in the face of outrageous acts like this, not to mention government restrictions during the COVID-19 pandemic on everything from business to church meetings (which I deal with elsewhere in this book). If I were an enterprising leftist, I would be gleeful at how willingly most Americans (even Christians and other conservatives) went along with every single restriction of freedom the government at the state and local levels forced upon them.

If Christians continue to yield at every turn, we may find our lives dictated by a set of elites who have no regard for the Christian way of life, let alone the American one. This was foreseen by one of the most astute Christian intellects of the twentieth century.

An Intellectual Prophet

The respected Christian philosopher Francis Schaeffer in 1978 gave what amounts to a remarkably prescient prophecy. He made a series of videos on one of his main messages, titled *How Should We Then Live?* On several of these videos, he predicted that elites in various industries and sectors of society would determine what everyone should believe—and enforce it punitively, just as they have begun to do.

"There really is only one other alternative left after the Christian consensus is gone," Schaeffer said. "And that is that a single individual, or a group will come forth as an elite, to give arbitrary absolutes to society. Now, we mustn't think this is extreme in our thoughts, because...many different kinds of people have made suggestions in just exactly this direction....Daniel Bell, who is one of the great thinkers of this particular moment of history, has written a book called *The Coming of Post-Industrial Society*. In it he says both government and business have become so technical that the techno-crats must become an elite to take over. And he says this is what's going to happen if we continue in a straight line from where we now are. But in it he gives a most astute warning—a warning that 'the lack of a rooted moral belief system is the cultural contradiction of the society, the deepest challenge to its survival.'"[5]

Then Schaeffer spoke words that ring eerily true today when American elites "rule" over what people can say or do via the airwaves, on the internet (which did not exist in Schaeffer's lifetime), or in the workplace: "You could sum up what he's saying, and brilliantly saying, as that in such a society, there is no absolute ethic to accompany the absolute power. That's exactly what stands ahead of us in this matter of an arbitrary elite taking over and giving arbitrary absolutes to the community. Humanism has found no way to deal with the problem of morals and ethics and values. Rousseau's romantic utopian theories led to the violence of the French Revolution and to the guillotine."[6]

My friend Chris Hodges didn't face a guillotine—but his mega-church was expelled from the public school buildings it had been renting because cancel culture reared its head in Alabama.

Hodges founded and leads what some say is the largest church in Alabama: the multicampus Church of the Highlands, with somewhere around sixty thousand members. He and the church could not be more accommodating or supportive of their communities. They feed the hungry, clothe the poor, and give education and work training to all sorts of people. They are not known as being confrontational about social issues. So when Hodges' church was ejected from renting public facilities in Birmingham, it came as a shock to many.[7]

The stated reason was this: Hodges, on his private social media account, had "liked" political posts that leftists opposed. That was it. He hadn't taken a new public stand against leftist-approved ideas. He didn't even make his own political statement. But someone who objected to the tweets he "liked" outed him. There was such an uproar over what some leftists considered unacceptable behavior it drew national media attention, and the school board responded by withdrawing approval for Church of the Highlands to hold satellite services in school facilities.

Church of the Highlands survived this brouhaha and has even grown in many other locations. Hodges acknowledges that he didn't build the facilities and it was the school board's prerogative whether to let the church use the buildings. But his example shows that cancellation now happens when you simply show approval for what someone else says that runs counter to the leftist agenda.

This type of cancel culture against the church is not just in America but in the UK as well. There, Jesus House church in northwest London was doing such good work in the community, especially during COVID-19, that the leader of the UK's Labour Party, Sir Keir Starmer, visited to applaud its community ministry efforts. Pastor Agu Irukwu and Jesus House have been highly supportive of efforts to educate the Black, Asian, and other minority communities about the COVID-19 vaccine. The Prince of Wales and Prime Minister Boris Johnson, among others, also visited Jesus House to see its vaccination center.

But when Starmer learned via a storm of social media posts from the LGBT community about the church's biblical stance on marriage—that God intends it to be between a man and a woman—he tweeted his regret and apologized for the "hurt" he caused by visiting the church's center.

Pastor Irukwu told the UK Evangelical Alliance that in a society like Great Britain's, "it is normal to expect that people would have diverse views, hence the need for a public discourse and debate. This sets a parliamentary democracy apart from a dictatorship where there is no discourse and rule by decree."

He warned of "the erosion of values like fairness and justice that are foundational to a healthy society. I am also concerned that incidents like this are indicative of a society sliding into intolerance of views and opinions that are different....As a pastor, I hurt for members of our congregation and other members of the larger church family, who on the most sacred weekend in our church calendar have been subjected to the most vile, abusive form of cyberbullying."

Somewhat forebodingly, Irukwu pointed out the obvious truth that "the Christian faith in some quarters is now seen as a soft target. Part of my stand on this issue is that I feel it is a concerted attack against the ideals of freedom of speech and freedom of religion which we all must protect....Having been through what we have experienced, I fully understand why the millions who hold to orthodox biblical teachings on marriage and relationships will be very reluctant to speak up and, in some cases, frankly afraid to do so. This is the result of a 'cancel culture' and the fear of...what has been described by British comedian Rowan Atkinson [best known in the US for his role as Mr. Bean] as falling 'victim of the digital equivalent of a medieval lynching mob, scouring social media for any evidence of indiscretion.'"[8]

"In the United Kingdom, we've got some challenges where if you want to believe the biblical model of marriage, then that is seen as not really fitting with a progressive culture," Gavin Calver, head of the Evangelical Alliance, of which Jesus House is one of thirty-five hundred member churches, told me. In view of this increasing global cancel culture, Calver (whose family I've known for thirty years) shared the word God gave him when he first took on his leadership role: that we need to be both braver and kinder than we've ever been, standing on an uncompromising faith and an unconditional love.

"So we're going to go out on a limb, but we're going to treat people well," Calver said. "In the UK there are...all kinds of stories where it's getting increasingly hard to stand for biblical truth. The organization I lead is absolutely committed to an orthodox interpretation of Scripture. And as such, you—from time to time—find yourself as a sort of cultural leper.

"But in the middle of that we stand for truth; we stand firmly on God's Word," he added. "And the challenge in the UK right now is not to change the Bible to fit your culture, but to believe that we can change our culture with the truth and the Word of God."

Calver said he personally experienced the impact of cancel culture when he tweeted out a review of a book that challenged biblical views on marriage. "In twenty-four hours, [I] got two thousand messages of hate from all kinds of people that would disagree with me, all kinds of horrible things, and praying that my kids have mental health issues…and all kinds of horrible stuff." One such message read, "You are the scum of the earth and are going to burn in hell. #love wins."

But even this hasn't changed Calver's "braver and kinder" approach. "In the middle of that, you simply say, 'You know, I am going to live for the approval of Jesus. And I would love my culture to love me. But right now in the United Kingdom, if you're going to stand for Jesus, then you're going to stand out, and the cost and the price tag are really high.'"

Calver added that amidst what seems like a dire situation, the doors for the gospel have opened wider than ever. This is true, he said, "because the church does not grow from the mainstream; it tends to grow dramatically from the margins. And we're being pushed to the margins, from where you have no nominalism left—you simply have people on fire for Jesus. And my hope and prayer [are] that radical remnant will lead to a revival in my nation, that will transform it into something it's never been: fully, fully surrendered to Jesus. But it's going to take a while. And it's going to take some guts, no doubt about that."[9]

I was also interested to learn that Irukwu publicly requested that his brothers and sisters "pray for more grace for us" and for "unity in the body of Christ." He asked fellow believers to "please pray that we will not grow weary in doing good and that despite all that has been thrown at us, we will continue to obey the injunction of our lord and saviour Jesus Christ to 'bless them that curse you, pray for them which despitefully use you' (Luke 6:28). We believe that God is working out His own plans and purposes and ultimately His name will be glorified."[10]

Prayer and support will be necessary because the attacks are becoming increasingly violent and unhinged. Another Christian pastor in the UK was told by the local police to keep his opinions in a "safe environment" because if he offended the homosexual and transgender community with a social media comment, he could be breaking the law. I learned of this through Christian Concern, a UK persecution watchdog. It reported on Pastor Josh Williamson of Newquay Baptist Church, who was targeted by sexual anarchists with a wave of anti-Christian abuse, including threats of violence and calls for his church to be burned down.

His crime? Williamson, who is thirty-five, replied to a post on a local news outlet's Facebook page that reported that Cornwall Pride, a pro-homosexual event, would be canceled. Williamson simply wrote, "Wonderful news!" under the post. When another user questioned him about his comment, he replied, "Because I don't think sin should be celebrated." Answering more questions from other users, Williamson quoted the New Testament's statements on homosexuality from the Books of John, 1 Corinthians, and James.

On his personal Facebook page, he shared the news article and wrote, "Hallelujah!! We prayed at our prayer meeting on Tuesday night that this event would be cancelled. We also prayed that the Lord would save the organizers. One prayer answered, now we wait for the second prayer to be answered."

After that post, Williamson's head was superimposed onto an image of homosexual pornography, which was then shared online. His wife also received online threats. Anti-Christian groups called their supporters to report him to the police for a "hate speech" crime, and some made threats to get the government to revoke the church's charity status. Some went so far as to threaten to have Williamson deported to his native Australia.[11]

Will Christians stand with people such as Irukwu and Williamson? Or will they submit to the great pressure to conform to the so-called elite's new morality? With truly remarkable foresight, Francis Schaeffer more than forty years ago said such pressures would become crushing for many Christians.

"The mass media can be used by an authoritarian manipulating government or an elite," he said in an era when most Christians couldn't believe this to be true. "The elite gives the arbitrary absolutes and then, not only TV but all the mass media can be used for manipulation. A plot or conspiracy is not needed. All that is needed is that the people in the places of influence and those who decide what is the news have in common, the modern results of humanism, the modern worldview....When the perspective, the worldview, of the elite coincides with some of the influential news carriers...then either consciously or unconsciously, the media becomes an instrument for manipulation."

But Schaeffer also believed people's desire for "personal peace and affluency" would "totally submerge" their resistance to being controlled.

"With most people, the young and the old, committed to apathy, and most of the populations of the various countries being committed to the values of personal peace and affluency, do you think they will stand up at great cost against such a trend, as long as they are promised the affluency and the personal peace?" Schaeffer pointedly asked.

"Will they not rather...give up even their liberties step by step, one after another, as long as they have the illusion, even the illusion of personal peace and affluency?...People with merely the values of personal peace and affluency would give up anything in the light of these pressures, especially if, in...our own day, as in the days of Augustus back in the Roman Empire...the changes were brought in while seeming to keep the outward forms of constitutionality. And with the growth of these pressures, modern man with his apathy, and with his desire for personal peace, will crush....That's just where we are," he said in the video series, which is well worth watching.[12]

Resist or Comply?

In February 2021 John Burton, a teacher, prophetic messenger, and revivalist who has been affiliated with the International House of Prayer of Kansas City, wrote an insightful op-ed on Charisma News titled "Big Tech Censorship Means a New Social Media Game Plan for Christians."

"In an era of muzzled speech and shadow bans, it's time for believers to wise up," Burton wrote. "We need to finally admit what has been true for years. Jack Dorsey, Mark Zuckerberg, Sundar Pichai, Jeff Bezos and the rest of the liberal tech and media decision makers control the narrative. These are leaders who have the right to promote or shut down activity that they deem appropriate or inappropriate for their respective businesses. The fact that their businesses are vehicles for our media makes no difference."

He made the point that these people don't realize they are being used as "puppets of a wicked, devious spirit that intends to mold society as it sees fit."

"My heart is grieved mostly because Dorsey, Zuckerberg, Pichai, Bezos and the others have not encountered the shock and awe of God's overwhelming, indescribable, supernatural love," Burton wrote. "Yes, the restriction of speech in our nation troubles me deeply. Yes, the rapid decline of godliness in our culture is gut wrenching. Yes, the corruption in the media, whether mainstream or social, can't be ignored. We are living in threatening times."

But for Burton, none of that compares to the reality of eternity. He added, "Heaven won't be the same without Dorsey, Zuckerberg, Pichai and Bezos."[13]

While these men and others have been busy influencing culture for years, my friend David Lane of the American Renewal Project says a turn happened when "corporate America became in 2015 the biggest promoters of same-sex intercourse and marriage. More than 350 companies, 'including Apple, AT&T, Staples and Target filed *amicus curiae* briefs urging the Supreme Court to strike down same-sex marriage bans.'[14] Yet citizens in 30 states had passed amendments opposing same-sex marriage, often by wide margins."

Shortly thereafter, five US Supreme Court justices took the place of God and invented homosexual "marriage," forcing every American to accept it by fiat.

"The Founding Fathers could not have fathomed what's happening in 21st-century America," Lane wrote in response to that and other happenings. "The upcoming battle about freedom of conscience will be with the secular and media luminaries who dominate the spiritual, intellectual, educational, economic and vocational cultural mountains of influence in America. 'Big Business' has become allied with the secular left, turning into active combatants attempting to put the final nail in the coffin of America's once biblically based culture."[15] How then do we as believers react to attempts at cancellation in the public square?

Balance Lane's view with Burton's, who reminds us that "the decision makers for our nation are, by and large, unbelievers. They live by an entirely different code of ethics. What makes sense to Christians simply does not make sense to them....Attempting to force our values on them will have no positive effect. Even if we are able to grab the reins, their hearts will not be turned to Jesus by brute force. Their resolve to resist what we'd define as righteousness will only grow stronger."

If we don't like their rules, he said, we can choose not to use their businesses.

"If I'm in a library and the librarian asks me to whisper, I whisper," he wrote. "If I'm visiting a church, I don't presume to be welcome to take the pulpit and preach. The businesses we are visiting make the rules. If a restaurant doesn't allow people to wear MAGA hats, they have that right. Christian bookstores don't have to order Harry Potter books for their customers, and secular bookstores don't have to stock Bibles. Their business, their platform, their rules....Yes, I agree that such a position by a massive facilitator of communication does put our American values at risk. But, unless the laws change, they have that right. Facebook can shadow ban, Twitter can suspend, Amazon can choose not to sell your book, Google can reject your app. They have those rights."

Burton's remedy is to ditch "the aggressive, bombastic and threatening disposition that so many on the political right (or left) have." Conspiracy theories, he said, "have to go."

"We can get the message across, in most cases, while honoring the place that gave us an opportunity to speak," he wrote. "We are guests on the various social platforms, and they have the right to uninvite us at any moment. Using Facebook and Twitter and the others is a privilege, not a right. Instead of feeding our addictions on social media by sharing every controversial, conspiratorial viewpoint that pushes you closer to the edge of a violation of their terms and conditions, why not play nice, stay inside their boundaries and advance the kingdom of God? Preach truth. Exhibit love. Let that be what drives you instead of anger, complaining and vitriol over politics and other hot topics."

With that said, Burton insisted he is "not saying we cower or compromise. Never. I'm saying there's a wise way to deliver your message without going over the edge and triggering those who have the power to shut you down."

But in his view, getting shut down is just a matter of time: "Social media is most probably going to shut down all Christians at some point. We just need to be smart by not expediting the process....Do I believe our speech as Christians will be ultimately restricted even further in the near future? Yes, I do. This is why we must come up with a strategy of advancing the gospel that takes this into account. The underground Chinese church has done it. Other restricted and persecuted groups of believers have done it. It's time for a social media underground movement to emerge. Until that happens, we need to tread carefully and respectfully on the surface."[16]

The founder of Gab.com, Andrew Torba, didn't kowtow to social media platforms—he built his own. Now, he says, we need to build our own economy. He wrote an outstanding article to that effect in early 2021:

> The oligarchs believe that they have destroyed American Populism by rigging an election, removing the movement's leader from public view, and by forcing everyone to stay locked inside for a year while the country burns down around us all.
>
> They think they have won and want to define "New Normal" under their rule as they consolidate power. What they don't realize is that they have recruited tens of millions of Americans to the side of reason, light, and Truth. Many millions of these people didn't even vote for Donald Trump, but they recognize what is happening to our country and want to stop it.

He went on to suggest something dramatic:

> The entire system is corrupt. Banks, tech companies, media companies, schools, government, and on and on. We must exit this broken and failing system and start building a new one immediately. We are not revolutionaries. We are not violent. We are reformers. We are builders. When we up and leave the existing system in favor of our own, (then) the existing system will crumble without us lifting a finger.

His list of ten suggestions for exiting the current system includes pulling money out of stock markets and investing in gold, digital currency, food, and ammunition; putting energy into local elections for mayors, school boards, state legislators, and judges; turning off all cable news and exiting Big Tech; leaving large banks for local banks; supporting small, local shops; homeschooling; and buying only brands that don't explicitly give money to leftist causes.[17]

Trevor Loudon, another bracing voice whom I discuss in more depth in the next chapter, wholeheartedly supports the approach of boycotting and "buycotting" to build up and tear down businesses according to their pro-freedom or anti-freedom support.

Loudon said we should abandon Big Tech en masse immediately. "Patriots should be abandoning Google, Facebook, Twitter, etc., for more honest platforms," he said. "They should also enthusiastically support efforts by [Florida governor Ron] DeSantis to heavily fine Big Tech operators who 'cancel' patriots. If 25 or 30 free states did the same, Big Tech would soon be little tech."

"Patriots," Loudon wrote, "need to organize nationwide boycotts of unpatriotic companies and buycotts for loyal American companies like MyPillow and Goya Foods." Equipped with lists of "unfriendly" local companies and better alternatives, "patriots can stop supporting their opponents and spend more with their fellow MAGA supporters."

Loudon even suggests sequentially targeting vulnerable unpatriotic companies. "Imagine if 80 million MAGA patriots resolved to begin a nationwide boycott of one such company, starting now," he wrote. "The boycott would go on indefinitely until the target company was broke, or it apologized for 'canceling' patriots.

"If applicable, every MAGA family could simultaneously commit to buying at least one of the canceled person's products this year. [Then] another disloyal company could be targeted, then another....After two or three companies had collapsed or apologized, we would soon see large companies start to back away from the 'Cancel Culture.' Patriots have spending power in this country, people. We need to starve our enemies and feed our friends. Again, patriots need to build a nation within a nation."

Many people think it's especially important to boycott anything made in China.

"Check those labels!" Loudon wrote. "Buying Chinese communist products in 2021 is like buying Nazi products in 1939. It's immoral and it's suicidal. The Chinese Communist Party just crippled the U.S. economy with the CCP virus. Then, pro-China communists instigated mass Black Lives Matter rioting. Then, the same people worked to influence the 2020 election. It's about time Americans stop funding their No. 1 enemy—the CCP."[18]

Beyond boycotts and buycotts, my friend Ken Fish, whom I

introduced in chapter 1, said American patriots must become better informed about history and political thought as we reject anti-American ideas in our midst and reinstitute basic American ideas.

"This is a time for people to read up," Fish told me. They need to read "books that normally are only read in better universities, so that people can become educated and understand what the issues are at a deeper level than what we can do in a podcast, or some preacher can throw out in a sermon, or somebody can create in some...video on Facebook. People need to become educated, and they need to start pushing back."

Polite, yes. Violent, no. "But we do need to be firm, and we need to become...unrelenting," he said. "I think the theological term is *perseverance*. We need to become as unrelenting about this as our opponents are."[19]

And we need to understand that what we're dealing with is far more sinister than just liberal versus conservative. We're seeing the emergence of a uniquely American form of communism: at best, frightening, at worst, murderous—to biblical values, to our way of life, and to individuals it deems "less than."

Chapter 5

IT'S NOT JUST CANCEL CULTURE— IT'S COMMUNISM

IT'S ONE THING to make choices in a free market. It's something else entirely to lose that free market and with it the freedom to choose. For many insightful observers, that is exactly the choice we face today: a rebirth of liberty or a tyranny that dominates society—even American society.

Eric Metaxas is one of my favorite authors, a modern voice who is speaking more boldly and more articulately than most. He is adamant that Americans have enjoyed liberty for so long that we no longer appreciate what liberty is. It's like a fish in water, he said. Fish don't know what water is—they just exist in it until, for some reason, it's gone. It's the imagery he uses in his newest book, *Fish Out of Water: A Search for the Meaning of Life (A Memoir).*

For Metaxas, this battle is personal. Americans aren't just losing liberties; they are ceding the public square to a nemesis that menaced Metaxas' own family: Communism. Eric's father is Greek, and his mother is German; both grew up in Europe during World War II and under the constant threat—or reality—of the godless, heartless Communism that followed.

"My parents...raised me to know that Communism is evil, that American freedom is glorious and wonderful and a treasure," Metaxas told me recently.

Metaxas' mother saw her beloved Germany come under Russian occupation and transform into the ugly experiment that was East Germany.

73

"[She] experienced the horror of Communism in East Germany," he said. "She saw the unbelievable propaganda of the communists and how they push people around. It sickened her to the point that she escaped Germany."

His father, further south in Europe, saw the communists attempt to take over Greece immediately following World War II.

"He taught me to hate Communism," Metaxas recalled. "I grew up with an understanding of how wicked Communism is and how bad things can get."

But while he was growing up here in the United States, he noticed his friends whose parents grew up in America didn't share this same passion for freedom. Rather, they seemed to shrug and take liberty for granted. By contrast, as a young man, Metaxas traveled to East Germany with his mother and saw the border guards, the dogs, and the barbed wire that defined the edge of the then-Soviet empire. He remembers thinking, "Wow, everything I've heard is true. This is the world's biggest prison. They're trying to keep the people in."

That background fuels Metaxas' anti-communist ardor today. One of his main concerns is how the Democratic Party has embraced communist ideology and driven all naysayers into the political wilderness. He talked to me about how the Democratic Party of yesteryear—of John Kennedy, Bill Clinton, and even Walter Mondale—no longer exists but has been taken over by Marxists.

"The Democratic Party has gone leftward over the decades, and it is unrecognizable from the party of John F. Kennedy," Metaxas told me. "Look to the nineties. Clinton signed the Religious Freedom Restoration Act. He understood that the government has no right to infringe on the religious liberties of Americans, that the government can have no part in that. Well, suddenly the party of Bill Clinton has become the party that says, 'We don't care about religious liberty. Religious liberty is just a dog whistle for white supremacy.'"

Voters, Christians especially, "have to discern the times," he continued. "We are living in a time where if you vote for a Democrat, you are not getting Jimmy Carter; you're not getting Bill Clinton.

You are getting people who are completely sold out to the darkest forces in our political life, forces that are economically disastrous. But that's the least of it....They are culturally hostile to the foundations of most Americans."[1]

It is useful to remember that the thirteen original colonies were concerned about ratifying the US Constitution unless it was amended with what they called a bill of rights. The Preamble to the Bill of Rights expressed the open suspicion of centralized government power that existed among many of the states. Here it is in its entirety:

> The Conventions of a number of the States, having at the time of their adopting the Constitution, expressed a desire, in order to prevent misconstruction or abuse of its powers, that further declaratory and restrictive clauses should be added: And as extending the ground of public confidence in the Government, will best ensure the beneficent ends of its institution.

In modern language, this means the states at that time simply would not hand over power to a federal government unless that power was explicitly limited in very specific areas. The areas they felt needed utmost protection were expressed in the first two amendments, which read in their entirety:

Amendment I

Congress shall make no law respecting an establishment of religion, or prohibiting the free exercise thereof; or abridging the freedom of speech, or of the press; or the right of the people peaceably to assemble, and to petition the Government for a redress of grievances.

Amendment II

A well-regulated Militia, being necessary to the security of a free State, the right of the people to keep and bear Arms, shall not be infringed.

In the last two amendments of the Bill of Rights, Congress again, with as much clarity as possible, removed power from the federal branches of government and reserved it for "the people" and the state governments.

Amendment IX

The enumeration in the Constitution, of certain rights, shall not be construed to deny or disparage others retained by the people.

Amendment X

The powers not delegated to the United States by the Constitution, nor prohibited by it to the States, are reserved to the States respectively, or to the people.

Yet the leftists currently in charge of large sections of the US government are completely out of step with average Americans who fundamentally accept the US Constitution, its amendments, and the Founding Fathers' vision of our country, Metaxas said. "That has led to the cancel culture, and if we don't stand up to it extremely strongly," he said, "we deserve what we get…and America will cease to exist."[2]

A Kiwi Viewpoint

Metaxas is not the only one shouting from the rooftops that the communists—after false reports about their global demise—are indeed coming for our nation. I was fascinated by an article in the *Epoch Times* by Trevor Loudon, a New Zealander who is passionate about what's going on in the United States.

Loudon is an author, filmmaker, and public speaker who for more than thirty years has researched radical Left, Marxist, and terrorist movements and their covert influence on mainstream politics. He wrote a book called *The Enemies Within: Communists, Socialists and Progressives in the U.S. Congress* and made a documentary called

Enemies Within. In his *Epoch Times* article "A New Zealander's 9 'Starter Steps' to Save America From Socialism," Loudon wrote:

> I've traveled to every state in the Lower 48 and have addressed more than 500 audiences across this amazing nation. My message has always been the same: The United States is heading toward a brutally tyrannical socialist revolution—and if America goes down, every free country follows.[3]

Loudon and I both live in Florida now, one of the more conservative large states, and when we spoke, he couldn't have been more emphatic. "We're in a revolution," he told me. "We're in a communist revolution right now."[4]

He quoted what Donald Trump Jr. said in 2019: that the 2020 election would be one of communism versus freedom.[5] "Not a lot of people took him seriously at the time; I hope they are now," Loudon said.

Loudon explained that the communist movement never died but experienced a major setback with the collapse of the Soviet Union in the 1990s. China, he said, has picked up that slack—with a lot more money than the Soviet Union ever had. He also said that US governmental and military positions are now stacked with what he dubbed "Marxist, pro-Chinese Maoists, people who have worked in Chinese organizations, Chinese media groups, Chinese academic organizations, people who have basically worked to bring down America for a very long time."

"We're swimming in communism," Loudon said. "If you can't name it, how can you fight it? How could we have defeated the Nazis in World War II if we never used the name Nazi?...No, this is [communism], and it's all around us."

He also observed that "the media has been a big part of this. The education system has been a big part of this. The gutting of the intelligence services, and even the police intelligence departments, has been a big part of this."[6]

How is this possible in America, the land of the free and the home of the brave, which has given of itself—in lives and trillions of dollars—to make the world safe for democracy? Political commentator Doug Wead says the so-called American brand of communism has lulled many sincere Americans into believing it would be healthy, not harmful.

"A lot of my friends in the United States who were Bernie Sanders fans and favored socialism for America would tell me, 'Well, American socialism is going to be different from Venezuelan socialism or Soviet socialism,'" Wead told me. "But the socialism that we see practiced in America on American campuses, for example, is very much like Soviet or Venezuelan or Cuban socialism in that one of the basics is to prevent a conversation, to prevent the other side from speaking."

Cancel culture, Wead said, "is an evolution...a stronger degree of Marxism."[7]

Cancel culture always evolves into something worse, these observers all believe. Loudon quoted a meme he has seen making the rounds: "Cancel culture is a dress rehearsal for mass murder."

"That's what it is," he said. "What did Hitler do before World War II? He picked out a certain group of people and demonized and canceled them, then ended up slaughtering them. I'm referring, of course, to the Jews, but the gypsies and other groups were also targeted. The same thing is happening today....Marxism [demonizes] anybody who stands up for borders, anybody who stands up for the Constitution, anybody who stands up for traditional Christianity or the principles that made America great, because America must be destroyed....That is the goal of the communist movement."

Loudon senses a pent-up frustration in communist movements because for much of the twentieth century they had a third of the world under their domination. America got in the way of their total takeover and drove the Soviet Union bankrupt in an arms race. The United States has kept communism in check for a century. The last thing between communists and total power is America—which is why to them America must be canceled.

"That's why the communists are ripping down statues all over the country," Loudon said. "That's why they're altering our history and demonizing the Founding Fathers. That is why they're shutting down…patriotic businesses—they want a pure Marxist culture in this country, and they will brook no opposition….If [you think] you can sit back and avoid this fight and sit in your church and keep your lifestyle and keep your job…you're delusional. They're coming for all of it. They seriously want to slaughter the opposition, and they're setting the stage for it now. If we're not going to fight back, we deserve what we get."[8]

Many Americans don't even realize that a key component of this attempted takeover has happened right under our unsuspecting noses. It takes the form of a pernicious idea called critical race theory, whose influence in education, media, and elite society is both pervasive and controlling.

Critical Race Theory Infiltration

Many young people may not know they are Marxists because they have been duped into believing they are fighting for racial justice. Such is the deception of so-called critical race theory (CRT), whose foundations are thoroughly Marxist and anti-American.

Rob McCoy, a brave pastor and former elected mayor of an influential city in Southern California, about whom I'll have more to say in a later chapter, says CRT bases every person's value on his or her victim status.

"Victim status is where you rise in points in this new cancel culture," he told me. "They believe the Enlightenment…scientific method, modernism is a White man's construct to keep the minorities down, so they've canceled anyone who would speak or try to be logical or would put forward an Enlightenment idea or anything Christian."

Of the lowest value as it relates to victimhood, he said, is a White male heterosexual Christian. Of the highest value in this new society of cancel culture would be a Black transgender female lesbian atheist. "The more [of a] victim you are, the more valuable you are and the greater your political force is to exert," McCoy said.

But behind CRT is a totally different motivation that has nothing to do with race or even gender, he said, contending in a way that reveals his deeper, spiritual insight.

Cancel culture "boils down to one thing: atheism," McCoy said. It is between what God says and what man says. "They want to take their sin that has enslaved them and they want to make it a victim identity," he said, "and they want to call evil good, and they want to call good evil. This is a battle for the hearts and the souls and the minds of men, and their weapon is the political arena."

Cancellation is merely the first step in propagandizing a generation in the way of godlessness, he said. Then he added, "A lie will never survive in the presence of the truth...so they must censor." McCoy's own YouTube channel has been shut down merely for addressing conservative ideas and solutions.

Atheists clothed in the sheepskin of social justice want to ultimately produce total chaos in society, he believes.

Those who teach critical race theory "don't want a one-world government; they want absolute and complete chaos...and utter destruction," Pastor McCoy told me. "It is demonic. [The devil] comes to steal, kill and destroy—he wants the church destroyed. He wants all morality removed." That may come in the form of communism or an oligarchy, McCoy said. But whatever form it takes, it's going to be "just absolute anarchy if they get their way because they're defunding the police. They want to create as much riot as possible...under the guise of social justice."9

Pull the lens back and ask which global nation would benefit the most from chaos in America. It's the one that happens to be fully Marxist—and champing at the bit to become the dominant world power.

China Behind It

Joel Kilpatrick calls China "the greatest cancel culture in the world right now."

"China is a cancel culture by definition," Kilpatrick said. "They control the internet; they control speech; they control visas; they control the prisons. [They use] facial recognition and video and social credit scores. This is *Nineteen Eighty-Four* come to life."[10]

I agree. Someone sent me a picture of a T-shirt that read "Boy, was I right, (signed) George Orwell." Of course, Orwell wrote *Nineteen Eighty-Four*, the famous fictional prediction of what life would be like in America if totalitarian trends continued. Now it seems even worse because China increasingly seems to call the tune and write the checks for American corporations, including Big Tech.

"Many of the big companies...have got big deals going with China," Loudon said. "China is driving this. [Corporations] have made the decision that China is going to be leading the world, and they have hitched their wagon to China. They're doing China's bidding by strangling the rest of us out of existence, canceling our culture, canceling our businesses, destroying our churches—whatever it takes."

Disguised as an American social movement, much leftist activism, Loudon told me, is a foreign-directed communist movement within our borders and bent on our destruction. Through power grabs and funding mechanisms, communist ideologues now control much of the Democratic Party, almost the entire labor union movement, most universities, the pro-homosexuality movement, the feminist movement, the environmental movement, and Black Lives Matter, according to Loudon.

"All of these are communist movements, but most Americans have no idea of this because the media is so much on the side of the Left and the FBI is so negligent that we hear nothing about it," he said.

Those movements were temporarily stymied during the Trump

administration. In 2018 Trump put tariffs on Chinese goods. China responded by declaring a "people's war" on America. That didn't just mean putting tariffs on American goods. It meant an all-out attack using any means available. In Loudon's view, China's response played out in 2020.

"They just stole your election, burned your cities, and wrecked your economy, all deliberately done, and there [were] no consequences," he told me. "What is to stop them doing it again in the future? Right now the Chinese are getting ready to…consolidate their power over the South China Sea. The Russians are getting ready to invade the Ukraine, and Iran is getting ready to nuke Israel. All of this has happened because you have basically Iran and China and Russia's friends in the White House now."

In his view, the leftists in power will move quickly in the form of "shock and awe" to pack the US Supreme Court, make both the District of Columbia and Puerto Rico states, make mail-in ballots compulsory across the country, and centralize power at a dramatic rate—all to try to cement their power for years to come. When they are finally able to destroy the United States military, "China then runs the world, China and their Russian friends," Loudon said.

His prognosis is dire.

"You're not going to be able to feed your kids, you're not going to be able to go to church, you're not going to have a career, you're not going to be able to disagree with the government, you're not going to have any freedom or prosperity if you don't stand up now," he warned. "You're going to have the same kind of lifestyle that they currently have in Venezuela…and Cuba. That's where we're heading."[11]

What galls Chris Reed, a young pastor about whom I will have more to say in a later chapter, is that those leading us down this road are on the so-called "tolerant" Left.

"The Left has treasured the reputation…of being the so-called tolerant Left, meaning they preach acceptance and understanding toward all people," Reed told me. "But yet the tolerant Left is not so tolerant to other points of view that disagree with their current one.

The tolerant Left is not so tolerant toward history and the people in our history."

He pointed out that the Left preaches that Americans should give up their Second Amendment rights—while leftist politicians walk around with armed bodyguards. The Left preaches that it's immoral for a nation to have boundaries—yet builds a barrier around the Capitol in Washington, DC, while many of its adherents live in gated communities.

The Bible warns such people that their deeds will come back on them, Reed warned.

"Cancel culture is exposing its own hypocrisy...and it always comes back to backfire on its largest advocates," he said. The Left's ideology is "so full of holes and hypocrisies," he added, that if ever there was a time for us to rise with boldness and courage and speak the truth in love, it's now.

A Way Out

Eric Metaxas, as many people know, wrote a best-selling book on Dietrich Bonhoeffer and is a serious student of Germany in the 1930s. I asked him, in light of the historical example his parents experienced so keenly, how cancel culture proceeds and what its stages are. He introduced me to a phrase coined by a German sociologist writing about the 1930s: "the spiral of silence."

"Chuck Colson picked up on that," Metaxas explained. "Somebody suddenly realizes...'Hmm, we're living in a time where if I don't say, "Heil, Hitler," my neighbors, my colleagues are going to look at me funny. So maybe I'm not on board with Hitler, but I'd better say, "Heil Hitler," because I want to keep my job.'

"Now today we think, 'Oh, "Heil Hitler," I would never say that,' but to say that in 1933 or 1934 was no big deal. Nobody understood that Hitler was going to murder millions of people. They just thought, 'It's a kind of a government we don't like, but we're going to go along with it...because I don't want to lose my job. I don't want my neighbors to report me. Maybe I'll be questioned by the Gestapo. I don't want that trouble. So I'll just go along.'"

The spiral of silence manifested when people ignored the fact that the Gestapo or SS or Hitler Youth were abusing a Jewish person, or some other injustice was done and they looked the other way. Every time they added another layer of silence to preserve their own skin, they made it much harder for people to stand up later.

"They were feeding the beast, and the beast was becoming more powerful," Eric said. "When you do not speak up, you contribute to the spiral of silence. It gets more and more difficult to speak up."

Comparing it with today, he said it was possible to speak out on behalf of biblically defined marriage as "one man, one woman for life" in 1995 or 2005, but to do so now invites much greater backlash and exclusion.

"You have a right to speak, even if your views are not what other people like...but the less we speak up, the more it contributes to the spiral of silence. And inversely...the louder and prouder and bolder you are, the more courage you have, the easier you make it for somebody to speak up."[12]

Such was the example of Dietrich Bonhoeffer, a theologian, prophet, and martyr whose life shines brighter today than it did in his own day. While Hitler's Germany began exterminating its own citizens and acting so belligerently that it caused a world war in which sixty-five million people died, Bonhoeffer and a few others worked at every level for righteousness and justice within that torn society. This even included plotting to assassinate Hitler, for which Bonhoeffer and others were shot or hanged.

The family of Corrie ten Boom, a friend and colleague of my most important mentor, Jamie Buckingham, also defied government orders by hiding Jews in the family home—an act for which family members were arrested and several died. Corrie later forgave her concentration camp captors and inspired tens of millions of people with her story of survival, mercy, and courage, told in her best seller *The Hiding Place*, which later became a movie. In later years she wrote *Tramp for the Lord,* which Buckingham coauthored.

Those examples, which happened within most of our parents' and grandparents' lifetimes, prove not only that we are never immune to history's ugliness but that speaking out and standing for what's right are always in fashion in God's kingdom.

Capitalism Restored

We must also stand and defend economic freedom, in addition to political and social freedom, Ken Fish told me. Paraphrasing the great free-market thinker Milton Friedman and his book *Capitalism and Freedom,* Fish said the simple fact is that political freedom arises from economic freedom, which protects people's ability to determine their own economic outcomes and means of production.

"Benjamin Franklin once said that a government that is big enough to grant you everything you want is also big enough to take everything you have," Fish said. "Ronald Reagan co-opted that line....This idea is as old as America. It's one of the reasons that capitalism is inextricably bound up with Americanism."

Certainly, capitalism has been done poorly at times, and there's a need to moderate excessive greed, Fish said. Then he added, "In the best case, the gospel itself should cause Christian businesspeople to moderate that because they should have the best interests of their employees at heart....

"Nevertheless...capitalism produces a greater level of wealth and therefore the greatest good for the greatest number," he said. "This is a direct reason why America is the wealthiest nation that has ever existed." It arose because "individuals [could] control the means of production and their own economic output and not be beholden to somebody...who had the ability to dictate what they did or didn't do."[13]

I agree that America is living proof—with more than two hundred years of history to back it—that capitalism gives more freedom than any other economic system. We certainly don't want to tear it down in favor of some alternate culture.

But what can be done to save freedom from Marxism? Some say the solution will be rather extreme—and violent.

Chapter 6

A NATION DIVIDED

ARE WE HEADED toward civil war? Are we on the verge of something like what America experienced in the mid-nineteenth century when millions of men went to war and more than six hundred thousand never returned, instead filling early graves over the issue of slavery and states' rights? Is this the future of our country?

Such a possibility does loom like a gray backdrop against the present scene, and more Americans are accepting it, even expecting it. Many levelheaded Christians are not just resigned to the fact of an impending civil war but calling for immediate preparation for such a thing. Rational, stable professionals I know have begun storing food and necessary items (Who wouldn't, after the 2020 toilet paper shortage?) in preparation of breakouts of violence or potential supply chain disruptions. Others I know personally who have never owned a weapon now carry a gun with a concealed carry permit. With thousands, maybe millions, behaving this way, it becomes difficult to dismiss as a fad or faulty assessment of the future.

It certainly does seem like two different Americas have formed within the borders of our nation. Indeed, this division drives cancel culture. The two Americas are so at odds over seemingly everything that some believe the only apparent solution is to annihilate the other viewpoint. Of course, this is not the America most of us grew up in, and the very discussion may seem jarring. But let's remind ourselves that during the Civil War era, those on both sides of the conflict built businesses and families, never expecting that their sons would go off to war and never return, or that their businesses and homes would be burned to the ground. How are we exempt from these same difficulties?

Having lived in a time of great peace and stability, many Christians—in particular the Charismatics I spend time with—are horrified by the suggestion that God would promote or even allow such a war. They seem to forget that America has been through wars before, which yielded righteous results, mainly freedom for our own citizens and for other nations.

Abraham Lincoln, who did not want to fight the Civil War but wanted to end the conflict as soon as possible while still preserving the union, became convinced that God was allowing it to drag on because the nation required a kind of bloodletting due to slavery.[1] Will rampant abortion, immorality, and injustice in America require a similar bloodletting in our day? Is war the cleansing crucible we must pass through to achieve greater national purity and unity on the other side?

Is it even biblical to think in terms of civil war, or should we take the posture the Quakers and others took in the previous one: outright pacifism? The Assemblies of God for its first few years (if not decades) was resoundingly pacifist. Today, its congregations and leaders seem to have no unified stance, nor do they desire one.

But is civil war just a popular, edgy thing to talk about, or are there actual indicators it is coming? Several credible spiritual leaders I have spoken with say there are.

The Second American Revolution

I spoke with longtime friend and popular author and speaker Rick Joyner about this and many other subjects pertaining to a potential violent conflict within US borders. Joyner has spoken frequently and with much specificity about the inevitability of another civil war, which he calls the "second American revolution," for at least the past decade. He has been trumpeting this idea because of a dramatic vision he received in 1987.

I wanted to know, How exactly do we prepare for a civil war—mentally, spiritually, and physically? What would this war look like? Would it involve bloodshed or control of major resources and things such as power plants, government centers, and so on? Would everyone be involved? Would it be physical, with guns and bayonets, or would it be a remotely executed, technical kind of war instead? Would it be about taking land or perhaps taking cyberspace? I asked Joyner about these many possibilities.

"Until a couple of years ago, I would have used the word *possible*. But I don't anymore. I think it's inevitable," he said of this civil war. "Some of my friends who thought I was crazy back in 2018 when I started saying, 'It's coming'—they now say, 'No, it's here.' They think we're already in it. I'm talking about pretty high-ranking military people. They think we've already entered a phase of it."

The source of his confidence, Joyner told me, is what he calls one of the most powerful and dramatic dreams he has ever received. In 2018, he said, he was shown that a second American revolution/civil war was coming. He was told in the dream, "It is inevitable. It is right. And it will be successful."

The dream revealed to him "America's history from heaven's perspective," Joyner said. To his great surprise, heaven did not think America had won the first Revolutionary War. In heaven's view that war was not just about gaining independence from the British but about "establishing a nation on the earth where there was truly freedom and justice for all."

"We won the independence, but...it became freedom and justice for some," Joyner said. "The slaves didn't benefit."

This failure to establish freedom for all Americans made the Civil War inevitable because the evil of slavery could not be tolerated any longer. But the Civil War did not accomplish all it should have, because Black Americans were still discriminated against.

"If the Civil War had done [its] job, we wouldn't have needed a civil rights movement and we wouldn't be dealing with a whole lot of this [racial] stuff that we're dealing with now," he told me.

Joyner began talking about civil war in 1987 when he was first shown briefly in a vision that America would go through a period of martial law. He wrote about it in his book *The Harvest,* and then he met well-known prophet Bob Jones, who died in 2014. Joyner said Jones also spoke often about the coming civil war.

"He knew how it was going to start and certain details about it," Joyner told me. "I always paid attention to [Jones] because I knew he was accurate."[2]

Jones related some of those details in a video recorded in 2010. In the hour-long message, given from an easy chair in a living room, Jones recounted revelations he said he received in the 1990s in a trance in Panama City, Florida. He dubbed the encounter "the perfect storm." It was a sevenfold vision of a future in which multiple forces converge to create a perhaps unprecedented time of confusion and instability in our country. The seven storms that would come together were, according to Jones: political/governmental, spiritual, financial, social, emotional, health-related (infirmity), and geophysical (earthquakes, volcanoes, tidal waves, and so forth).

"You're going to see a shaking in the government like you've never seen before," Jones predicted. This would cause America to reexamine its foundations and invite God's influence into political and civic life again. "We were born of the freedom of religion," he said. "I believe you're getting ready to see religion come to a new liberty and a new freedom like we've never seen before."

But first, a huge storm would come to the United States, "one of the biggest that we have ever seen. And it had many different facets to it," Jones said. One facet involved illnesses that, though not more serious than the ones that came before, would terrorize nations. Remember that Jones spoke these words a decade before COVID-19.

"The newscasters are scaring people like never before," he said in the video. "I don't believe that the infections and the flus and everything else that's out there now is really any worse than I've ever known them. I've seen really bad seasons when they were bad before, only we [weren't] terrorized by them. We lived through them. We went through them.

"But there's a fear that's being put out there by some of the newscasters," Jones added. "I think they are really your new terrorists. They're not giving any hope; they're giving you fear. If these things are frightening you, then turn that television off, that radio off. Put that paper down and go to Him who can give you peace. Infirmity? Yeah—let the redeemed of the Lord say so. If they say no, then it's going to be no. The world [doesn't] have the say. Neither does the devil; neither [do the devil's] people. But the saints have the say. And it's time they begin to come together and say, 'There'll be no influenza. There'll be no pestilence.'"

Jones also saw new blights coming to crops and wiping out vast acreages of genetically identical grains, for example. But to the point about civil war, Jones characterized the fifth storm he saw as "very dangerous" because it involved people's emotions and reactions to losing all they had invested their lives in due to societal turmoil.

"People are going to lose it [emotionally]," he prophesied. "They have invested their lives in retirements, in education, and laid their money back for the future. I think emotions are getting ready to go bananas. I think that some of your psychiatrists are going to need a Christian to deliver them." Only the gospel would bring them into a place of peace and calm their emotions, "to show them hope in a time of great disaster, to focus them on the light, and to focus them on the true absolute, which is the Lord Jesus Christ," he said. "The church has no right to...let their emotions get out of control, for they are the ones [that are] called to help others get them back under control."[3]

But for Joyner and others who believed Jones' message, the question remained: When would it happen? Joyner's own urgency came only with the 2018 dream. From that point on, it has become his primary message—and a popular one. The first printing of Joyner's book *The Second American Revolution/Civil War* sold out immediately when it released in early 2021. That may mean we are entering, or have entered, a perfect storm, he told me.

Again, I wanted to know from Joyner what a potential civil war would look like. Would it be a shooting war, like the one from 1861 to 1865? Would mass numbers be involved? Would it be physical, with guns and bayonets, or a technical, remote kind of war? Would it be aimed at taking land or taking cyberspace?

"We need to put out of our mind the [first] American Civil War when we think about what's coming," he told me. "What I saw was... going to be between the Left and Right; it was mostly going to be in cities. And I did see some of what was going to unfold. I saw cities; it looked to me like the entire cities were burning."[4]

Joyner has said elsewhere that he thinks combat will be from house to house, neighbor against neighbor, within cities, not in pitched battles in open fields with large weaponry.[5] This agrees with what prophetic people such as David Wilkerson have said for years. Wilkerson was given visions of cities such as New York on fire, torn by rioting as society broke down because it rejected God.[6] Even International House of Prayer of Kansas City founder Mike Bickle, who says he has received just two open visions in which he observed a spiritual revelation with his natural eyes, had such a vision in 2008. On what appeared to be a kind of screen in front of hi6m, he saw tanks roaring across America.[7]

In 2020 a little-known Kentucky Assemblies of God pastor, Dana Coverstone, suddenly gained an audience of over a million on social media and YouTube because of his "Brace yourself" dream and subsequent dreams, which contained details about potential catastrophic happenings in Washington, DC.[8]

John Paul Jackson, who died in 2015, said in 2008 that the Lord led him to speak strongly and repeatedly about what he, like Jones, termed "the perfect storm."

"I am delivering this message with a heavy heart," Jackson said. "This nation is about to undergo a great shaking. It will not be confined to the United States alone, but it will strike the greater global community.....Few, if any, will escape some measure of this shaking. What is coming is not what some might call the wrath of God.....It is simply a time when mankind has made a series of historical wrong choices."

Greed had corrupted business, and money had become the driving motivation in many churches, he said. Perversion, abortion, and sexual infidelity had reached critical levels, even among believers. The storm he saw ahead had five elements: religion, politics, economics, war, and geophysical events. He expected these to be so intertwined as to be indistinguishable at times.

"Massive problems in these five areas will come often, or in combination, and sometimes repeatedly," he predicted in a professionally made video, still available online. "Different areas of the United States will experience different severities. Some will experience more economic elements, and others more geophysical elements; some will experience all the elements. Remember, it is the combination and the rapidity that will make the storm problematic." (See note 9 for the link to the video.)

One prediction we seem to be experiencing now is the loss of God's protection of our borders. "Without God's intervention, they will become porous, and evil nations will bring broad devastation even to smaller communities and propagate fear on a scale never known in this land," he wrote in a companion booklet. This perfect storm would not be short-lived, he said, but would come in waves.

"This storm is coming because the Church (the Body of Christ) is no longer the backbone of this nation," Jackson wrote. "Money is seen as the sign of success and anointing. Money has become a driving force. It directs far too many churches that have monstrous financial needs in order to pay for facilities designed to impress the worldly system it should be trying to change.....We must prepare for severe change, for violent winds are coming."

Jackson said the perfect storm would force a decision: "Evil will become more obvious and righteousness will be tried and tested. We will have to make a choice—either darkness and evil or God's light."[9]

Another voice that caught my ear is that of Donna Rigney, a prophetic woman and copastor with her husband of a nondenominational church in Salt Springs, Florida.[10] She gave a Sunday morning word to her congregation on September 8, 2019, that she believes God intends for the church at large.

"A great war is coming to your land," she said, quoting what she said God told her. "All I could picture was armies coming and invading our land. 'This war will be different than what you expect.' So God was telling me, 'What you are thinking it's going to be is not what it's going to be. It will not be another nation invading yours, but it will be a war fought from within. Your foe is causing great dissension and strife, brother fighting against brother. His purpose is to stop the great revival from being birthed and advancing. He will not succeed.'"

Rigney said God went on to tell her several times, "'Mobilize the troops.' This is my job, this is our job: mobilize the troops. He said, 'Mobilize the troops, daughter. Holy Spirit will help you. Pick up the weapons of your warfare. I have trained My army well to use their most effective weapons: love and forgiveness....Through prayer you will see those who hate what stands for good and are blinded by deception turn to Me and embrace My way. Teach My children what I have taught you. Show them how to pray with love, compassion, and forgiveness for those who have sought to destroy, divide, and demolish their nation from within.'"[11]

On March 27, 2021, Rigney said the Lord told her enormous change was coming that would bring good to those who love God but destruction to those who resist Him. She saw "a lot of chaos in the United States. And I saw people that were getting buckets of cold water" with ice floating in it "thrown in their faces. And they were completely shocked when this happened."

What was happening? Rigney called it the time of birthing of the "child of revival," which the enemy has tried to stop. The birthing process would be "very chaotic, just like when a woman's giving birth," she predicted. "He was showing me...these buckets of water being thrown in people's faces. He said that what's going to happen during this time of birthing is there's going to be a great unveiling of what has been going on. Evil will be seen as evil, and good will be seen as good. People that believed that other people that were leaders or people they emulated and really looked up to and were heroes to them, they're going to find out they were not who they thought they were....We're going to see things as they really are. Truth is going to come forth."[12]

Preparing for War?

If all this is even a possibility, how do we prepare for it? As Christians, the obvious first answer is to pray.

"I think that, with extraordinary grace from God and wisdom, the damage, the casualties, or whatever we're headed for can be lessened," Joyner told me. "I think that's what most of those revelations are for. [God] needs intercessors on the earth to intercede for these things.... Our job is now to pray and maybe to take action that would prevent the bad thing from happening. Repentance and revival [are] usually the way we escape certain things."

While he does not believe we can build fortresses, compounds, or distant retreats where we can be physically free from everything that's coming, Joyner said the will of God will be the only truly safe place on the planet. For that reason, "we've got to resolve...to absolutely obey, seeking first the kingdom with every major decision, being sure we're even living in the right place," he said. "If we chose where we live based on geography or family or anything other than putting the kingdom first and seeking God first...we probably are dealing with many problems that are completely unnecessary in our life, because we're not in the right place....We've got to get these things right."[13]

I was heartened that Joyner put spiritual things first, because if we don't, having all the food and water and other resources won't help. In the natural, having those things might simply invite thieves to your home. But with God's blessing on our preparations, they could be great tools for sharing the love of Jesus when people need Him most. The perfect storm may provide the perfect opportunity to live and share the gospel.

But Trevor Loudon strikes a warning note about any talk of violence. He wrote:

> Violence will not save America. The harsh reality is that President Barack Obama had eight years to replace patriotic generals with left-leaning political appointees. He did a great job. If violence breaks out (God forbid), the military will stand with the government, not the insurgents. Does anyone think Russia and China and Cuba and North Korea and Iran would stand idly by while their Democratic [Party] friends are being defeated by a patriotic uprising? They would undoubtedly use the opportunity to finish off their "main enemy" once and for all.
>
> Beware of anyone inciting violence online, at a public gathering, or in a private meeting. Distance yourself fast. They will be at best hopelessly naive, at worst government provocateurs. The left is praying for "right-wing" violence. It will give them an excuse for a massive crackdown on patriotic Americans. This country will be saved peacefully or not at all. If significant violence breaks out, it's over.[14]

If you don't believe Loudon's words, just consider what happened after George Floyd's tragic death in May 2020. While his death by Derek Chauvin kneeling on his neck for nine and a half minutes may have been at random, it was sadly inevitable that sooner or later a White officer would kill an unarmed Black person. Of course, some Black officers occasionally shoot Black suspects, there's too much crime against Black Americans, and each death is tragic. But there are those on the Left whose narrative is that the *only* lives that matter are those lost at the hands of White law enforcement officers.

Those who hold to this narrative were ready when George Floyd was killed; they were waiting and organized, and they sprang into action almost immediately when the videos of his death went viral.

That's not to say much of the reaction by ordinary Americans wasn't spontaneous. Everyone who saw the videos should have been repulsed and angered. But there are stories of rioters being bused into urban areas, and the rioting that followed the release of the videos was almost immediate. Don't tell me that wasn't planned in advance!

Meanwhile, the Left looked the other way at the rioting and at times seemed to encourage it. While the rest of the country was in a virtual lockdown, rioters could gather in large groups with or without masks and with no regard for social distancing, and this was called "protesting" instead of rioting. It was even applauded by people such as Gov. Gavin Newsom of California, who at one point told rioters, "Those that want to express themselves…God bless you. Keep doing it. Your rage is real."[15]

Then, on January 6, 2021, when the US Senate was voting to confirm electoral votes for Joe Biden in the presidential election (that many, including me, believe was stolen), huge crowds converged on Washington to "petition the Government for a redress of grievances," to quote the First Amendment to the Constitution. But these Americans, who had a very different agenda than the Left, were portrayed by the media and leftist politicians as radicals coming to overthrow the government. Unfortunately, some were violent, and sadly, five lives were lost. But I'm told by friends such as Pastor Caleb Cooper from New Mexico, who attended the January 6 rally, that from where he was standing (far from the violence), all he saw "was worship and prayer surrounding the Capitol grounds—a sea of patriots who had filled the stairs of the Capitol suddenly started singing the National Anthem in unity."

I have been told that radicals, wearing "Make America Great Again" hats to blend in to the crowd, were the ones breaking windows in the Capitol to make the supporters of Donald Trump look bad. I can't verify that, but that's partly because no one will investigate. Those in positions of power to investigate seem to be on the side of the Left. In fact, during an event the day after what the secular press called an attack on the Capitol, Biden said, "They weren't protesters. Don't dare call them protesters. They were a riotous mob, insurrectionists, domestic terrorists....No one can tell me that if it had been a group of Black Lives Matter protesting yesterday, they wouldn't have been treated very, very differently from the mob of thugs that stormed the Capitol."[16]

At one point early this year, more than twenty-five thousand troops as well as barricades and barbed wire surrounded the Capitol. I did not see it, but close friends who were there told me our nation's capital looked more like Venezuela than America. And the reason: the same Democrats who seemingly saw nothing wrong with rioting and burning—in not one but many major cities and not just one afternoon but week after week—were suddenly warning that right-wing protests could become violent. Why else was it necessary to surround the Capitol with barricades and barbed wire and thousands of troops?

I don't advocate any violence except in the case of self-defense. And I believe the unrest on January 6, while not justified, could have been trumped-up (no pun intended). But at any rate, the hypocrisy of the Left in almost applauding violence perpetrated by its side while trying to make the Right look as though it was trying to overtake the Capitol is astounding. A friend in Washington, DC, who has seen many sit-ins and protests said the Capitol Police routinely admit protesters to the Capitol and let them stage a sit-in, say what they want to say, and then leave peacefully.

Point to note: the Right (and really anyone concerned about the direction of the country, whether political or not) should be aware that leftists are waiting for *any* excuse to crack down on those who oppose them, especially if violence of any kind is used.

After warning against violent rhetoric, Trevor Loudon added: "Having said that, the Second Amendment must be preserved at all costs. An armed populace is at least some check on tyranny, even if useless in the face of biological warfare or nuclear attack. Americans should keep their guns and work every day to ensure they never have to use them against their own people."[17]

Joyner also often counsels people to arm themselves so they can defend their households, which he believes is our biblical responsibility. In fact, he believes the First American Revolution and the Civil War of the 1860s both ended too soon because of political motivations and thus failed to thoroughly establish their purposes.

"If we've got to fight again, we've got to fight to win," Joyner said. "We are not going to tolerate injustice; we are not going to tolerate discrimination [racial or religious] or any of these things in our land."

When we finish the task, Joyner said, heaven's words will come to pass: "It's inevitable. It's right. And it will be successful."

"What does successful look like?" he asked. "From heaven's perspective, it has to do with our national destiny, which…is to be a place where there's liberty and justice for all, where all people are truly treated as equal under the law. And we're going to fight until that's finished."[18]

Every one of the prophetic voices quoted in this chapter predicted a time of great rejoicing and freedom breaking out after any potential civil war. John Paul Jackson promised that "after a period of time what is of God will remain and grow stronger as a result."[19]

Rick Joyner saw the emergence of what he called "a third column" of leaders with such wisdom and insight that they would unify the nation under righteous leadership.[20]

Bob Jones went further and into more detail. "I believe you're getting ready for spiritual authority on a level that's unimaginable," he predicted. "I believe we're in a time of change like the church has never known before….None of us know what's really going to take place because He hasn't revealed it before. And I think one of the reasons He hasn't revealed it is because we don't have anything in our past to relate to it. This is going to be totally new. And it's going to be the children of light really shining to give the children of darkness an opportunity to come to the light."

Home meetings, Jones said, would become powerful places of spiritual encounter and equipping of believers, unlike anything we have seen before. Leaders would grow in-home meetings and begin reaching thousands. Virtually all believers would begin to live in the reality of Psalm 107:2, quoted here in the Modern English Version: "Let the redeemed of the LORD speak out." Jones applied this to speaking the truth of God to civic life, spiritual life, and even weather patterns. New inventions and cures would be found. Families, cities, and entire states would come together in unity of faith in the Lord. Even nations would dedicate themselves to Him. Such was his vision of how the perfect storm would take Christians to a place of higher experience and authority. He called it our "finest hour."

"It's no time for the church to have fear whatsoever," Jones said in the 2010 video. "It's time for them to begin to rejoice because there will be souls coming in like they've never seen before."[21]

Jackson said in 2008 that Christians must declare sacred assemblies and corporate fasting nationwide. "We need change, deep transformational change, both personally and nationally," he implored. "We need the [awe] and presence of God back in our services. For this to happen, we must have broad, national repentance. We must cry out with godly sorrow, asking God to forgive and remove our mental strongholds that have alienated us from Him. When this happens in the heart of the people, we will change and pass laws that will reflect the righteous convictions based on our Creator's design and we will believe what we print, 'In God we trust.'"

Jackson offered six ways to weather the coming storms: not overreacting to media hype and spin, simplifying and streamlining our lives, reconnecting with friends and family, rethinking our focus, being an influence in the culture, and taking more time to listen in prayer. He liked to quote something he said the Lord told him: "Little battles produce little victories and result in little champions. Great battles produce great victories and result in great champions. Which do you want to be?"[22]

If the civil war vision of our future is true, perhaps we are in a kind of pause, a place of preparation before economies are disrupted and populations are drastically affected. But do answers exist—and are there battles to be won—in the political arena? While many sincere Christians and conservatives have given up on current systems, a number of leaders are still fighting for our freedoms in the political realm—and calling for others to join them.

Chapter 7

THE POLITICAL BATTLEFIELD

Ventura County borders Los Angeles County to the north-west and boasts a rural vibe, a far smaller population, and plenty of horses and hillsides. The county has a history of championing freedom and conservatism—the Ronald Reagan Library is located there, in the city of Simi Valley—but during the mass hysteria surrounding the COVID-19 outbreak, Ventura County became ground zero for bizarre and heavy-handed responses by unelected health bureaucrats. That overreaction set the stage for a handful of local leaders to take a stand for civil and religious freedoms that vaulted them to national attention.

Rob McCoy was serving on the Thousand Oaks City Council and had been the mayor of this city of more than 125,000 residents that sits on US Route 101 between Los Angeles and Santa Barbara. Thousand Oaks has often been ranked in the top four safest cities in America but has had a couple of difficult years with the recent wildfires and the 2018 mass shooting at the Borderline Bar and Grill, which left thirteen dead.[1]

McCoy is an unusual figure in that he not only excels in the political sphere but also is the pastor of Godspeak Calvary Chapel in the city. For years, he has exhorted Christians to become more involved in politics lest they lose their influence—and their rights. When COVID-19 hit, initiating a kind of mass hysteria throughout the country, McCoy quickly found himself in a dogfight for civil and religious liberties right in his own town.

Godspeak Calvary Chapel, like most churches, complied

voluntarily with government guidelines for the first few weeks, when the severity of the virus was unknown. But as it became clear that it was a relatively tame illness and when ultraliberal California governor Gavin Newsom declared churches were not essential—but abortion clinics, cannabis distributors, and liquor stores were[2]—McCoy was nettled. To make matters worse, Newsom did this before the first Sunday of the month, April 4, when Godspeak was planning to serve communion.[3]

McCoy and his elder board decided to hold a communion service anyway while following all CDC standards. "We wanted to put…forward that we're essential," McCoy told me recently. "The governor has no right to silence the church. None at all."

In this age of fear and instant outrage, his church's private, voluntary decision caused a firestorm of protest that even landed the church in the international press.[4] McCoy knew the city council on which he served would not defend him based on the US Constitution, to which members had sworn allegiance. It would instead censure him for going against the public guidelines—so he called the city manager and the other council members and resigned. It seemed McCoy had lost his political career and given up a place of public influence to stand on principle. It was admirable, but where would it lead?

Within days the people of the community voted with their feet. Thousands began attending Godspeak, whose sanctuary has about four hundred seats. Communion on that first Sunday took more than three hours to serve because of the number of people who showed up to receive. The press descended on the place and seemed poised to paint the church as super-spreaders whose reckless decision would kill half the community, the elderly in particular. But that prognostication proved entirely false.

The only outbreak from that meeting was one of insanity by Ventura County leaders, who began to threaten the church with fines and legal action. This caused even more people to flock to Godspeak, which for months was one of the few churches in the county meeting in person. While thousands rallied to the cause of freedom of religion and assembly, a county public health official began a strange, cock-eyed rampage against basic constitutional liberties.

Joel Kilpatrick, who lives in Thousand Oaks and has forged an alliance with McCoy and others to fight for freedom both locally and nationally, said Ventura County's public health agency has seen its annual budget swell over the years to hundreds of millions of dollars, primarily funded by federal and state grants.[5] This means the state and federal governments essentially usurped local control of health issues.

"The county hires a bunch of people based on all that grant money, and to renew that grant money and not have to fire people, they have to keep doing what the state tells them to," Kilpatrick said.[6]

While Godspeak was growing exponentially, Dr. Robert Levin, an unelected county public health officer—who makes nearly $300,000 a year[7]—started holding press conferences to talk about his plans to forcibly isolate infected people, taking them from their own homes and putting them in unspecified alternative housing.[8] He also cheerfully talked about placing thermometers on normal citizens to track them around town to source outbreaks. Strangely, he even gushed about wanting to experiment with testing local sewage for the virus because apparently it is detectable in public sewage. The idea was to trace outbreaks back to specific parts of town.[9]

Where were the Ventura County supervisors while this madness was being spouted?

"They scattered like cockroaches," Kilpatrick told me. "They quit meeting in person, quit being accountable to the public in any real way. They are not up to the job....[Instead], they empower these public health officers who are not responsible to the voters."

Many county officials feel cowed by Sacramento, where California's current governor is known to be especially punitive. He is up for a recall vote in the fall of 2021, about the time this book releases.

"He's a vindictive man," said Kilpatrick, who knows leaders who work with Newsom. "They tell me he's a Rehoboam, not a Solomon. Rehoboam was the king after Solomon, and he was vindictive toward the people and wanted to punish and control them....That's Gavin Newsom's character. If a city votes against him, he will come after that city, no matter how small. If a county goes against what he is dictating from Sacramento, he will come strongly against that county and try to strip them of funds."[10]

The once freedom-loving Ventura County did not even attempt to defend its residents. Instead, it rolled over and tried to enforce the state's weird, draconian rules. I heard about this all the way in Florida and during the pandemic interviewed both Kilpatrick and McCoy on my *Strang Report* podcast because it was one of the worst examples of government overreach.[11] And while the restrictions affected only the residents of Ventura County, they had nationwide implications since if these actions went unchecked, other officials might follow suit.

Kilpatrick and McCoy began making noise in their circles of influence. Kilpatrick was the first to call for Dr. Levin's firing or resignation. Levin responded by mocking those who were "into Constitutional rights" and might try to put "blockades" in front of his ideas. Within days national media took notice, and he and the county were held up to scorn on Fox News' *Tucker Carlson Tonight* and many other platforms.[12]

Still, the county persisted in harassing churches, businesses, and private citizens, threatening fines, closures, and even arrests. "We were blown away by how quickly public health was weaponized against free citizens and against the free exercise of religion and speech and... assembly," Kilpatrick said.[13]

Arrested in Florida

I was told by Mat Staver of Liberty Counsel that my friend Rodney Howard-Browne, who founded The River at Tampa Bay in Florida, was the first pastor in the world to be arrested for opening his church during the COVID-19 pandemic and the first pastor in American history to be arrested for the offense of holding a church service. To the credit of Florida governor Ron DeSantis, less than two days later

DeSantis issued an executive order declaring attendance at churches and places of worship an essential activity. He then overrode every local order and freed churches throughout the Sunshine State.

But for McCoy, the pressure worsened and became truly Orwellian. In August 2020 the county sharpened its knives and came after Godspeak again. McCoy had given up his elected position, but he gained a much larger national platform as a true freedom fighter. He began touring the country with Charlie Kirk of Turning Point USA and stumping for the reelection of Donald Trump.

Apparently, Ventura County supervisors felt they needed to put McCoy and the entire church back in their places—of subservience to government mandates. Three of the five supervisors voted to use county money to hire an attorney and seek a temporary restraining order against the church and McCoy personally, empowering authorities to arrest not only McCoy but also the first thousand congregants or visitors who disobeyed the order. Then they were to have the sheriffs enforce the order, possibly locking the church building and arresting McCoy and a thousand attendees.[14] A judge approved the order, citing "an immediate threat to public health and safety due to the 2019 novel coronavirus."[15]

"Mind you, we had been open wide since after...the LA riots occurred [on May 31, 2020], and the governor praised BLM Inc.," McCoy told me. "Seventy-five percent of the businesses that were burned and looted were Jewish-owned and targeted, and the looters did it without masks or social distancing—and the governor praised them. We knew this wasn't about science or medicine. It was about power and politics, so the supervisors tried to exert their force on us, and so we violated that restraining order."

McCoy and Kilpatrick showed up at the church that Sunday knowing they and many others could be arrested, that McCoy could lose both the church and his house, and people could go to jail. But when they arrived that morning, "it was the most amazing thing," McCoy said. "Churches from all over California...and Western states drove to our church and surrounded our church. When I walked in, they said, 'We're here because…we're all in agreement. We're going to get citations so that you and your congregants can worship in peace.'"

But while these Christians were voting yes for freedom, nearly all other pastors in the area were voting no.

Months earlier, when word spread that Godspeak was considering holding its communion service, "a number of pastors called and said, 'You're going to be a detriment to the gospel, and you're going to ruin our reputation in the community. Please don't do what you're going to do,'" McCoy told me. "The body of Christ was divided. And I told them…'You guys don't understand. From a pastoral perspective, you think that peace is the absence of conflict. But not only am I a pastor; I also hold office, and I know exactly what these elected officials are attempting to do. So I'm going to move forward with the knowledge I have, and you can join me or protest against me. But I've chosen clearly; I've weighed the choices.'"[16]

I wish I could say the reaction of these other pastors surprised me. It's hardly a secret that many pastors are passive and don't want to be criticized. As I've written before, in my forty-five-year career as a Christian journalist, I've observed many pastors who are not true leaders. They go into ministry for other valid reasons—maybe they have a counseling gift or perhaps a teaching gift, or they just love people.

We want pastors who love people, but many have no real backbone. In these times we need strong spiritual leaders who are willing to take a stand. Part of my reason for writing this book is to make this point, hoping pastors who read it will wake up and see what is happening not only to our country but to the religious freedoms most Christians take for granted.

I witnessed this passivity firsthand when I supported Mike Huckabee for president in 2008. Huckabee is a godly man, a former Baptist preacher—truly a dream candidate for conservative Christians. He was lieutenant governor of Arkansas and became governor when the former governor, Jim Guy Tucker, was convicted on conspiracy and fraud charges in the Clinton Whitewater scandal.[17] Huckabee served for ten years and did a great job as governor. I thought if ever a conservative Evangelical could get elected, it was Huckabee.

I did everything I could in my circle of influence to rally support for him, including raising a whole lot of money for his campaign. But I ran into near-total apathy on the part of pastors, who seemed hesitant to publicly support a gifted Christian brother who was capable of winning elections and governing well. That opened my eyes to the fear pastors and nonprofit leaders feel when it comes to entering the political realm.

The Paper Tiger Johnson Amendment

The so-called Johnson Amendment has been used by many Christian leaders as a get-out-of-politics-free card. This threatening but innocuous 1954 amendment to the IRS code said a church or nonprofit organization would be stripped of its tax-exempt status if it got involved in politics.[18] Since 1954 only one pastor has been audited (not punished) by the IRS for violating the Johnson Amendment,[19] but this threat hangs over the heads of churches and pastors—or at least they pretend it does, so they hide behind it rather than speak out on political or social issues of real importance to the people they lead.

The Johnson Amendment is so bogus that for years, some churches have purposefully publicly endorsed candidates and alerted the IRS that they were doing so. They wanted to provoke a court case that would cause the law to be tossed out as unconstitutional. But the IRS, apparently knowing it would lose that case, has refused to enforce it.[20]

Still, McCoy's experience highlighted this distressing fact of pastoral reticence, and I mentioned to him that I never thought I would live to see the day when churches were attacked by government officials. McCoy—who is clearly savvy and experienced in the political realm—was quick to point out my naivete.

"That is the blind spot for the body of Christ in America," he said. "Fifty years ago, we abdicated the public square. We don't participate in politics anymore. Our voter turnout is...pathetic. Pastors no longer engage in political discourse and conversation; they justify it by saying, 'I just preach the gospel.' I hear that all over the country when I travel: 'I'm not political; I just preach the gospel.'...But they've avoided conflict. They think that peace is the absence of conflict, and it's not. Peace is the presence of Christ in the midst of the conflict."

McCoy pointed out something else that is well worth considering—that is, when Jesus said He would build His church, He used the word *ekklesia,* which means public square or congregation.[21]

"He didn't use a religious term...He used a secular term that had been used hundreds of years before Jesus co-opted it," McCoy told me. "Jesus said, 'Upon this rock, I will build the public square, and the gates of hell will not prevail against it.' Greeks used to meet in the *ekklesia,* which was their town council. And above the door of every *ekklesia* were two words, *isonomia* and *elutheria,* which meant 'liberty' and 'equality.'...[The public square] is exactly where the church is supposed to be because from moral law comes civil law."

Not only that, this modern statesman told me, but Jesus instructed us to make disciples of all nations—and nations have boundaries and constitutions. "The church has abdicated stepping into the public square....That grieves the heart of the Lord," he said. "Pastors aren't prepared to contend with [things like critical race theory and immigration]....We don't participate in city council....The church is being decimated and played like a useful idiot because they say, 'We don't do politics.' And that is exactly what the church should be doing. Aristotle said politics is the highest form of community. It combines morality and sociability.[22] Everyone does politics...and it's about time the church wakes up to its responsibility to impart moral knowledge. And from that will come civic laws that point people to Christ.... We've got to wake up. There needs to be an awakening."[23]

While McCoy, Kilpatrick, and others were fighting their county health officers, forty-five minutes away in Pasadena my longtime friend Ché Ahn at Harvest Rock Church was facing the same sort of harassment from a city. Ahn and his church were racking up huge fines and facing intense legal and social pressure to shut down because of the city's order restricting home Bible studies and prayer meetings. Ahn stood his ground and soared into even greater national prominence when his lawsuit against the state made it to the US Supreme Court—and he won. But until that victory came,[24] Ahn and McCoy—two potentially historic American leaders—didn't have many other pastors standing with them in the public square championing basic constitutional freedoms.

They did, however, have a strategic ally in the California state Capitol—a self-described tongue-talking, Jesus-loving veteran named Shannon Grove, who as state Senate minority leader was the highest-ranking Republican in this state of forty million residents.

"The Government Is Coming After Our Pastors"

You may have heard the saying "As goes California, so goes the nation." California state senator Shannon Grove of Bakersfield began to raise the alarm early on so the rest of the nation would realize what was happening in the state known for its extreme liberal slant on almost every topic. Because of the restrictive stance Gov. Gavin Newsom took, Grove said churches and pastors faced true persecution; their freedom to worship is under attack. But she and many other Christians stood up and spoke out in defense of our First Amendment rights.

"We have churches where the governor is telling people how they can worship, how long they can worship," Grove told me while these restrictions were still in place. "He says, 'No singing and chanting,' which means worship and prayer....He says no instruments that are horns or that use physical exertion and air to be able to blow through. He says that everybody must wear a mask. He says that you have to open at 25 percent capacity. He's telling not only worshippers and the church how to worship; he's telling them when they can worship and how they can worship."

Beyond that, the governor's policies were pummeling families, she said. "You have people that are unemployed…1.6 million people still not receiving benefits from the…unemployment office [since] he took their job away," she told me. "The churches are essential, and they should be partnering with government, and government should be partnering with them to fill those gaps and fill those holes.… Wholeness and counseling and things that the church can offer would be beneficial to those that are hurting in the state of California. But the governor is not taking that route. He is hostilely attacking the churches."

Grove boldly spoke at Sean Feucht's Let Us Worship event in Sacramento in September 2020—only to see Governor Newsom impose more government restrictions, many believe as a retaliatory measure.

"They estimated eight thousand people showed up at the California state Capitol to worship the Lord, and it was led by Sean Feucht, and pastors were making declarations, and prophetic words were spoken over our beautiful state," Grove told me. "And the governor actually put out a guidance on those types of gatherings just because of what Sean Feucht did that day with those pastors. So now it is against the guidance and against state policy for the Department of California Public Health to have any type of those gatherings like we had as a worship service to protest the governor not allowing us to worship. So it just keeps going further and further and further away from what God's values are."

She said Newsom didn't even give pastors and churches the opportunity to help create guidelines to keep people safe. Instead, "he just said, 'No, you cannot operate,' and what he did say was that they could operate in a certain percentage of capacity based on the county they're in, which made it very difficult."

Grove, the longtime owner of a temporary staffing company with locations in four cities, entered politics only at God's direction. After having served in both the California Assembly and Senate, she stands solidly behind the churches that defy unconstitutional orders.

"I'm very, very proud of over twenty-eight hundred churches that opened May 31 [, 2020,] and said, 'We are worshipping our God, and you're not going to tell us how to do it,'" she said. "Now some of those churches you've heard about in the media—John MacArthur, Rob McCoy, and many others that are being persecuted by their county governments and the state government—they've been dragged into court; they've been fined....The counties are coming after our pastors, and the government is coming after our pastors. And what's really sad to recognize is that it's not being shown in the media. And if people understood that pastors were being persecuted in this way—that they were being fined, that they were being threatened with jail time, that they have to have attorneys to defend them to preach God's Word and to just operate as a pastor in a church—I think America would wake up, because that happens in countries where you have no religious freedom and religious rights and you don't have a Constitution that protects you. It should never be happening in the United States of America."[25]

Bethel Church

A couple of hours north of Sacramento, in the mountain-ringed city of Redding, one of the most influential churches of our time was experiencing California's mega-crackdown as well. I asked senior leader Bill Johnson what it was like to pastor through 2020, especially with a government so hostile to churches. I was curious to hear his view on how to stand with the government in its God-given role yet defy unjust rules and laws. How should Christians resist being canceled while still respecting the authorities?

"It really is a crazy season, an unexpected season," Johnson told me. "We have been really warned of the Lord to really get into the system, not being afraid of politics, get in and serve well. It is strange to have the church considered nonessential. And we have worked really hard with our local authorities to do what is responsible in this pandemic but also to maintain the values that we have, as leaders [and] as a church family. And we've walked in good standing with the city and good counsel with the health leaders. They sometimes differ from the governor, which has been helpful for us, but we've tried to be responsible citizens but also responsible for the Lord, to love and to serve people well."

He pointed out that the government's reaction to COVID-19 caused a whole slate of harmful effects, including depression, financial issues, and all kinds of strife in the home under the mandated lockdowns.

"It's just insanity," he told me, "that this would be logical to our government. And so it saddens me to see these decisions made, but I am encouraged that many believers are rising up, not just verbalizing what they don't like but actually providing solutions."

When Sacramento took such a hostile posture toward churches, it put Bethel Church in what Johnson called "a strange position" because the church had "created a momentum of discipling a city for many, many years, and we felt a responsibility to pay attention to our civil leaders."

Churches with less visibility could get away with meeting in person and ignoring guidelines—but many eyes were on Bethel, which highly values partnering with governments and honoring their position in society. "We felt that our responsibility was to follow the policies the best we knew how but also to make our presence known and to train our people to have their meetings in homes," Johnson said. "We ignored all policies that said people couldn't meet in homes and that sort of thing. We actually worked hard to support and to…fuel or empower the people to meet in homes, and we've had tremendous breakthrough as a result."

Johnson said they felt corporately that God was asking them to humble themselves and go back to their raw beginnings of holding prayer meetings in a tent even in inclement weather—which is exactly what they did, setting up a tent and meeting in the cold of winter, night after night.

"We had…meetings and prayer meetings and…[times of] crying out to God," Johnson said. "The glory of the Lord has come in ways we've not seen in a very, very long time." He said they felt that the Lord was "reestablishing some of our foundation." He pointed to the *Rocky III* movie, in which the trainer told Rocky, "The worst thing happened to you that could happen to any fighter: you got civilized."[26]

"Sometimes you just can know too much and be too accustomed to comfort," Johnson said. "And we felt that we were just supposed to humble ourselves, return to the sawdust trail, so to speak, get in this tent, no sides to the tent, very cold, very challenging conditions. And yet we showed up; hundreds and hundreds and hundreds of people would show up day after day after day and cry out to God, and it really has provided a breakthrough for us."

Bethel had an enormous online audience of more than half a million regular viewers before the pandemic, and that number shot higher during the lockdown. Johnson said reports of conversions, miracles "galore," and unusual stories of changed lives keep pouring in from online viewers.

"All kinds of amazing things happened just through an online service," he told me. "We've had to relook at what God is ready and willing to do. I've always believed He could do it, and somewhat would do it, but never to the level we've seen this last year."

By the way, Bethel has not been canceled by YouTube, though both Bill and Beni Johnson have had social media accounts restricted due to posts on their personal accounts.

"For a season, we had many in our teams, our pastoral staff, their stuff has been taken off of Instagram or Twitter or whatever....That's happened to a lot of our folks," Johnson told me. "If you make any kind of a post that maybe supports Trump or maybe supports the Supreme Court relooking at the voter election fraud issues, or any of those kinds of things, they can shut you down and just say it's against policy."

What is happening at Bethel Church and many other places is the reason I wrote this book. Johnson continued: "If you say something against maybe a bill that's up before Congress or Senate...they'll call it hate speech or something, even if you just present facts, even if you're not lashing out at anybody, not accusing anybody....It's really crazy what they can get away with. They have a power that nobody has had before in the history of our country to control what people hear and what people read. It's really, really quite sobering. And we've got to wake up as a country because this is it."

With the Supreme Court wins for churches, Bethel, like thousands of other churches, is back meeting in person and moving toward full capacity while keeping in communication with the City of Redding.

"[The City of Redding] is in a tough place because they're under the pressure from the government in Sacramento," Johnson said. "We're trying to honor them but at the same time take care of our people. So we've been working on both ends of this thing. And while we've not always chosen what I would do...I've had to listen to the counsel, the advice of our teams, and I feel like we've done well....I have very little respect for some of the decisions that government has made just on a personal, individual level. But it can't be about my opinions; it has to be about what's best for our church and what's best for our city. And I think we've made it through that storm well. I'm shocked at how well we've done, and the people have been so responsible and so diligent."

At the same time, he added, "We're also at the end of our...tolerance of that mandate and are diligently pursuing—with counsel, with wisdom—how to get the group back together."[27]

While churches such as Bethel pursue their kingdom mandate to honor governments and kingdom principles, some Christians wonder if it's even worth participating in politics anymore. How does one participate in a political system many believe is hopelessly compromised, corrupt, and weighted against conservatives? Why do so many self-proclaimed conservative politicians fold and go along with liberals once in office? Haven't conservatives been dragged around by the nose, fleeced, and taken for granted for fifty years or more by Republican politicians?

Rick Joyner said the current political system has suffered exactly what our first president, George Washington, said would happen: that political parties would end up destroying the republic.[28]

"I think that...there shouldn't be any political parties; we should be able to debate any issue just being Americans," Joyner told me. "So many major decisions have been made on political expediency rather than on what is right, what is constitutional....As much as possible, [I want] to be delivered from any political spirit, anything that would ever cause me to compromise what is right, what is true, just for what is politically expedient.

"I want to know the Constitution. I read it all the time. I want to understand it. More than that, I want to know the Bible. [Charles] Spurgeon said he could find ten men who would die for the Bible for every one that would read it. I think that's still the case. People are so loyal to the Scriptures and the Bible in theory, but they're not loyal enough, in many cases, to even read it, know what's in it."[29]

Trevor Loudon, the America-loving Kiwi, proposed several solutions when I spoke to him about answers to the most serious challenges bedeviling our nation. First off his lips were the words "election integrity."

"Election integrity...is absolutely essential because our side now is so disgusted with elections, a lot of us don't vote," he said. "That's what we saw in Georgia. You've got two Marxists in the US Senate from Georgia now because a whole bunch of Georgia Republicans were so disgusted and dispirited by the steal of the election, and the absolute gutlessness of the Republicans to fight it, that they stayed home. Well, we're going to see that happen all over America in 2022 unless the thirty red states get very, very tough about election integrity....If we don't do this, we're going to lose virtually everyone in 2022."

He stressed the needs for stiff penalties for organized voter fraud—suggesting fifteen-year jail sentences. The problem will go away "very, very quickly" with that kind of consequence, he promised.

I experienced a possible instance of voter fraud in my own family. In Florida you must present your driver's license or voter registration card when you go to vote. We have paper ballots. During the early voting window, I picked up my then eighty-eight-year-old mother, who had moved into assisted living and was in a new precinct, and drove her to the polls. When we arrived at the polling place, they told us, "She can't vote. She's already voted."

My mother has some level of dementia and forgetfulness. She said she couldn't remember if she had voted, but I knew she had not; she did not have the ability at that point to fill out an absentee ballot and mail it in. I found myself standing there, unable to prove she hadn't voted, so they turned her away. I suspect somebody went through and voted absentee for all the elderly people in her assisted living center. I wrote to the supervisor of elections in my county but never got a reply.

"They wouldn't do that if they'd go to jail for fifteen years," Loudon told me when I shared this story with him. He then alerted me to the presence of an organization that he asserts is run by a pro-Chinese communist group. The organization, he said, is dedicated to "flipping" states from red (conservative) to blue (liberal) because leftists are friendlier to communist regimes.

"They are committing all sorts of acts in this state [Florida] to flip the state," he said. "You've got to have a very vigorous effort on behalf of state governments to weed out these organizations that are communist-controlled, working for communist China to flip states in the American South. They've already flipped Virginia. They're on the verge of flipping North Carolina. They've already partially flipped Georgia. They've already partially flipped Arizona, and Florida is right in their targets, and so is Texas. They only need another one or two, and the Republicans can never win nationwide again. It's that serious. We need law enforcement involved in this in a big way."

Next on his list of reforms is the abolition of voting machines—whether or not they were rigged. His reasons: "Our side will still not have confidence in them. They will still not believe it. They want to see paper ballots and registration and photo IDs. Then they will have confidence that the election is fair, and then they will vote. Until those steps are taken, we're going to lose."

Loudon's suspicions of corruption ring true to me if for no other reason than what I have observed in Florida's elections. We have a solid, conservative governor, Ron DeSantis. He led well through the COVID-19 mess and opened Florida before governors of other large states did the same. But he almost lost the 2018 election, although we have two Republican senators as well as a Republican House and Senate. Democratic candidate Andrew Gillum, the Far Left mayor of Tallahassee—a total unknown—almost beat him. In such a strongly Republican state, how did that happen?

Alliance of Free States

Loudon then proposed an idea that seemed radical on first hearing but made sense the longer I considered it. I am sure he is not alone in proposing it, because I have started to hear other versions of it discussed by intelligent, in-the-know people. It is this: to create a formal alliance between the thirty red states so they work together to oppose the federal government. These would include Florida, Texas, Louisiana, and the rest of the Deep South (perhaps minus Georgia), and the Plains states, Midwest states, Idaho, and Alaska—"from Alaska...all the way to...the Florida Keys," Loudon said.

He described their partnership as "a bloc—not secession—a nation within a nation" that would comprise most of America's workers, wealth, and food. "You basically tell the federal government, 'You are not going to do anything unconstitutional in our states,'" Loudon said. "'You're not coming for our guns; you're not coming for our religious liberties; you're not coming for our elections; you're not coming for our freedom of speech.'"

"The Tenth Amendment guarantees that states are superior to the federal government," he continued. "The federal government serves at the pleasure of the states," and the US Constitution guarantees states a republican form of government. If the federal government tries to take away that form of government, "the states have a right to band together and tell them to take a hike," he said.

He even proposed that red counties in blue states could join this voting and economic bloc. In the here and now, governors Ron DeSantis of Florida and Greg Abbott of Texas are already designing legislation to fine Big Tech if they suppress conservatives.

"Imagine if thirty states got together and said, 'We're going to fine Google and these companies a million dollars a day each if they keep suppressing freedom of speech....Make it five million dollars a day,'" Loudon said. "Big Tech would be Little Tech really, really quickly."[30]

As part of that process of clarifying the role of states with regard to the federal government, Loudon also proposed a rigorous review of the relationships between the federal and state governments, which he calls a "republic review."[31] Some western and northern states are already agitating to review their relationships with the federal government, to disallow unconstitutional aspects.[32] Up for inspection would be the many federally funded programs in areas such as health and education that hamstring or dictate policy to states, counties, and cities.

Shadow President?

Loudon encouraged people to follow President Trump's lead when he asks people to boycott entities such as Major League Baseball, UPS, and Delta Air Lines, which publicly opposed voting reforms in Georgia.

"If 80 million MAGA people boycotted those three or four companies, the cancel culture would be gone pretty darn quickly," Loudon said. "We have the power; we are the majority; we have the money. Our people work; our people have businesses. Stop giving money to our enemies and start giving money to our friends."

This includes boycotting China in every possible way.

"Read your labels; don't buy any Chinese goods....Don't have shares in any companies that invest in China at all," Loudon said. "Investing in China today is like investing in Nazi Germany in 1938. You're building up the enemy that is going to kill your kids if they get the chance. Spend your money with American companies. Buy American; buy patriotic."

He counseled every family, individual, and group to have a list of the "good" companies in their areas and nationally, and also the "bad" companies that support organizations such as Black Lives Matter.

"If we directed our resources to our friends and against our enemies, we could end cancel culture," Loudon said.[33]

Church as Champion

Back in Ventura County, a judge refused to let the supervisors force the sheriff to arrest McCoy and Godspeak attendees. But McCoy said the county continued to send "spies" who attended services and made notes on what they deemed violations. It was also startling to see McCoy required to show up in court for his hearing—answering for merely exercising his private liberties as the leader of a church.

In that court hearing, the county health officials' hypocrisy was brought to light because they didn't realize the church had been observing them while they were on church property. One even per-jured himself. On cross-examination, Godspeak's lawyer asked if the county official followed the standards he was enforcing or noting that church attendees did not follow, such as social distancing and wearing face coverings, including when standing outside. The county employee claimed under oath that he did.

Godspeak's lawyer then presented him with a photo in which he was standing in the church parking lot with his mask hanging from his ear. He also showed a photo of the other two county officials sitting in their car together, both maskless, not socially distanced.[34] But instead of dismissing the officials' testimony and canceling the order, the judge found McCoy and the church in contempt of the order, though he reduced the weekly fine levied against Godspeak from $1,000 per incident to $500 per incident. "I fully understand that there's a reason that freedom of religion is protected by the very First Amendment. But I have a duty to uphold the Court's order that was duly issued," the now retired judge said, adding that the church's "willful disobedience" was "well-motivated."[35]

Godspeak was now drawing people from hours away by the thousands. The church went to four services and packed out every room in their facility. Elders began looking for a satellite campus as the church became a place people would call, asking if there were churches like Godspeak in their own states.

Meanwhile, the county was losing steam—and McCoy wasn't budging on principle or paying the hundreds of thousands of dollars in fines the county demanded. "I told them, 'I'll see the inside of a jail cell before you're going to see a dime of that money,'" McCoy told me.

Finally, the county dropped its suit entirely, giving up any attempt to reap unjust fines from McCoy or Godspeak church.

How then can Christian people resist cancellation at the local level, as McCoy and Kilpatrick and many others around the country have done? Cancel culture is hitting cities and towns of all sizes as leftists feel emboldened to go after anyone who raises a voice against their agenda.

"Real simple," McCoy told me. "There's way more of us than there are of them."

One way of doing that is by starting a freedom-friendly newspaper where Christian and conservative viewpoints are welcomed. "We couldn't get the newspaper to print truth," McCoy said. "They were owned by the cancel culture. And so was the editor. So we started our own newspaper, and we stand up."

He also counsels direct, nonviolent confrontation.

"Contend with cancel culture and…give them what they gave you," he told me. "You meme them. You meme what they're doing, and then they cry, and you meme them while they're crying. That may sound cruel…but the reality is you must tell the bully to sit down. They may not like the fact that they have been confronted with their sin and that they have to look it in the eye and they're going to be treated that way. [But say], 'Now sit down,' and they do. You push back; there are more of us than there are of them, and their behavior is unacceptable. And they must be corrected. It's not acceptable in society. Don't turn a blind eye, and you don't walk by quietly while they're ruining everyone's life."

Most of us have heard the famous quote attributed to Edmund Burke that says, "The only thing necessary for the triumph of evil is for good men to do nothing."[36] But if we do stand up, is it possible to restore America through present institutions such as city councils and federal elections?

"It is possible to change the country," McCoy said. "One man and God constitute the majority. I can show you everywhere in Scripture where it changes overnight. He pointed to 2 Kings 7, where Elisha prophesied to the king during a devastating famine that there would be an abundance of grain the next day. "[The king's officer said], 'Even if the heavens opened up, there would be no such an abundance of grain.' And the next day, God provided it."

He then quoted from the famous Old Testament verse: "If My people, who are called by My name, will humble themselves and pray, and seek My face and turn from their wicked ways" (2 Chron. 7:14).

"Their wicked ways are apathy," McCoy said. "Their wicked ways are turning a blind eye to the decimation of a million babies a year. If they would turn from their wicked ways of the fear of man being a snare, and being more concerned with their social popularity on social media [than with the scourge of abortion in this nation], 'If My people would turn from their wicked ways, *then* I will hear from heaven and heal their land.' God can change it, and yes, politics is a wonderful way because that's the public square. That's the *ekklesia*. That's what it's supposed to be."[37]

Chapter 8

PERSECUTION IN AMERICA?

WHAT IF WE prayed ourselves into this persecution?

When early Pentecostals—including my own parents and grandparents—prayed for global revival, part of the answer seems to have been the amazing revival in China, which happened under severe and violent persecution, imprisonment, and chilling social control.

Now that same persecution seems to be coming to our shores. For example, the framework for a Chinese-style "social credit" system is being laid here in the United States at an accelerated rate. Social credit systems are a type of cancel culture and persecution. We see these systems arising in America through

- online and cell phone tracking,

- people being fired from jobs for social media posts simply expressing mainstream political views,

- the snitch culture, which is rising fast (see, for instance, the Nextdoor website),

- facial recognition software,

- the tracking of COVID-positive citizens, and

- church registration during the pandemic.

Each of these ideas is antithetical to freedom but has become acceptable in mainstream American thought in the last eighteen months. I grew up thinking our country would always be exempt from this type of control, which happened in some third world and communist countries, but the landscape in the land of freedom is rapidly changing. Some Christians are saying cancel culture is only a stepping-stone on the way to something much worse—a Chinese or North Korean style of totalitarianism that currently enslaves a billion-plus people.

Are we becoming a country in which Christians—and people of other religions—are harshly persecuted? Is that God's plan for the coming days?

A House of Prayer in the Midst of Persecution

It's not especially popular to predict that sustained and difficult persecution is on the way for Christians, but Mike Bickle has never been one to hew to popular notions just for the sake of being positive. The founder of the International House of Prayer of Kansas City, Bickle believes persecution of the church in America has already arrived, with some believers feeling it more and some less, and that it will increase "dramatically" in the coming years. More alarmingly, he told me in a recent interview, "It's biblical that it's coming."

I asked what could possibly be biblical about persecution. He pointed immediately to Psalm 2, which is the subject of many of his messages and of his book *God's Answer to the Growing Crisis*, which Charisma House published in 2016. Bickle says we are living in the first few verses of Psalm 2, prophesied by David three thousand years ago, in which the kings and rulers of the earth come into greater consensus than at any point in history to remove God from society. Bickle defines "rulers" as influential leaders in various arenas of culture, such as academia, the media, politics, the marketplace, finance, the military, sports, and entertainment.

"They're going to plan and scheme…[to] drive the influence of the Word of God out of the culture," Bickle said. "To the secular mindset, God's Word is bondage and it stifles our human potential—old, archaic laws in the Bible that are keeping us back from our full potential in sexuality and spirituality and everything else....[They are going to] get rid of and dismiss the Word of God in the public square in every way possible. That has really accelerated in the last twelve months and then much faster the last twelve weeks. It's almost at a breathtaking speed," he said in early 2021.

Bickle pointed to an obvious but easy-to-overlook reason this is happening now: the internet. "Without an internet there could not be thousands of people emboldening one another with crazy ideas," he said. "The internet has given...accessibility for all kinds of people to voice their opinions and...validate and embolden the people that are like them."

The ability to communicate instantly and globally in mass numbers is indeed a completely new opportunity for humanity that became possible only within the last couple of decades. Most people don't consider how revolutionary this has been for society.

"All of us have multiple devices of one kind or the other, and news and information and opinions [are] coming in so fast at everyone," Bickle said. "People who would have never thought of certain things are now not only thinking about them; they're enraged about them, and they see themselves as experts on them."

It occurred to me as a publisher that the Reformation itself likely would not have happened had Gutenberg not invented the printing press. Martin Luther was not the first person to criticize the Catholic Church the way he did, but people who did so previously, such as Jan Hus, could not disseminate their messages easily around the world because printed books did not exist. Technology allowed the rapid spread of ideas and caused a global change to the church.

In Bickle's view, we're seeing the same dynamic happen today—a modern outworking of an ancient impulse that took place at the Tower of Babel in Genesis 11. At that time, humanity began to unite spiritually and culturally against God, but God intervened to stop their progress toward a full manifestation of wickedness because it wasn't time yet. Now, Bickle said, God will allow the full flourishing of wickedness, empowered by the ability to communicate without hindrance. He called the internet "the global unified language" and said the day of near-instant translation between people speaking different languages is almost here.

This is fueling the spread of the gospel—but also the spread of evil.

"At the end of the age, right before the Lord returns, the human race [will enter] into a realm of darkness beyond anytime of history and interaction with demons," Bickle said. "That is, I think, what was being talked about in Genesis 11, touching the heavens, and that's happening now."[1]

An Angel Predicted Explosions of Travel and Knowledge

There is another fascinating aspect to this, and it's found in Daniel 12:4, in which an angel predicts two specific things about the end of the age: knowledge and travel across the earth will greatly increase. The angel said it this way: "Many shall run to and fro, and knowledge shall increase" (Dan. 12:4).

My grandfather A. R. Farley was a Pentecostal preacher in Kansas for more than fifty years. His daughter, my mother, who is now ninety-two, still tells how he preached in the 1930s about Daniel 12:4. This was before the age of widespread air travel, computers, television, or the internet, so he was mainly referring to automobiles, trains, and of course print media. My grandfather could not have envisioned the internet or the fact that today you can reach people by cell phone and not even know they're halfway around the globe. (I once called a local friend, and when he answered, I discovered cell towers had found him in a matter of seconds in Argentina, where he was visiting.)

Bickle has done extensive personal study on the totality of human knowledge (which we might also call "information") and said the increase is staggering—and accelerating. Some estimate that it used to take a thousand years for all human knowledge to double. Then it took a hundred years to double. Then it took twelve months to double.

Now, with artificial intelligence and computer technology, some say the totality of human knowledge doubles every twelve hours.[2] There is no sure way to quantify this, but if you include all information created daily in the world—every email, text message, photo, article, audio recording, video, and so on—it comes into focus. In my own career as the owner of a publishing company, we have published two thousand books and many more magazine issues—and that doesn't include our massive amount of online content. In our company's own small way, we have contributed to the rapid increase of information and communication.

The point is, in one brief, seemingly cryptic phrase in the last chapter of the Book of Daniel, the main features of our day were foretold—twenty-five hundred years ago. It has "massive implications [for] the spread of evil as well as the spread of good," Bickle told me.

The angel in Daniel 12 also said travel would increase. I remember growing up during the space race. In about one hundred years the world went from the invention of the combustion engine to putting a man on the moon—a phenomenal fact. Today, millions travel by air without even a thought, when the very idea would have boggled the minds of our great-grandparents.

But what does this mean for the possibility of persecution? Bickle said the ease of travel greatly enables the spread and coordination of evil plans among "kings and rulers" and their followers who are determined to rid society of God.

"A guy can be in London, then be in New York…in seven hours," he said. "The heads of state and the rulers of the culture…can be together so easily, whether they're physically together or through technology, and the Tower of Babel evil is multiplying because they're all sharing their experiences, their information. And they're emboldening each other and approving and applauding. And then the masses of the earth are hungry for more of it."[3]

I asked presidential adviser and author Doug Wead what he thought about the possibility of persecution.

"The first thing that comes to my mind is…I don't think Americans are fully prepared for how bad it can get," he said. "They keep thinking, 'No, no, no, it's not going to happen. It's not going to happen.'…Technology is certainly available now with chips and tracking [to] keep accounts of everybody. As we know, in China right now, you can't get an apartment unless you have a high [social credit] score. It has nothing to do with how much money you have. It has to do with your score with the government. If you're caught jay-walking, that's a knock against you. Of course, if you are a member of a Christian church, it'd be a knock against you. And so I'm sure that's going to come to the United States. In fact, it's American companies that have implemented that for China and are providing that for China. Truly, truly astounding."[4]

Ken Fish sounds a similar note. "I try to maintain an optimistic view of life, but…right now, people that think the way you and I do, do not hold the high ground. We do not hold the levers of power," he said to me. "The cards are stacked against us."

He continued: "We have our work cut out for us. Anybody who thinks that this is all just going to go away on its own is probably whistling past the graveyard."[5]

Antichrist Approaching?

Many Christians naturally take the next step and wonder if we will see the rise of the Antichrist and a one-world government in our generation.

In the Pentecostal circles I grew up in, the end-time was a big topic of conversation. Everybody had a theory about when things would happen, in what order, and what it would all look like. Some had big charts and pointers, and they would indicate when they thought the rapture was going to take place, when the great tribulation would happen, and so forth. I tended to be like a preacher friend who joked that he was not a pre-, mid-, or postmillennialist but a pan-millennialist—because he thinks it's all going to *pan* out in the end. Many of us who sat through hours of presentations of end-time scenarios with charts and timelines and headlines indicating where we were in history probably ended up feeling that way.

Charles Crismier, founder of Save America Ministries and author of *Antichrist: How to Identify the Coming Imposter*, believes the new world order is looming—and that the church is playing a huge role in setting the stage for the Antichrist.

"The problem is a combination of...lack of trust and...disobedience," Crismier told me. "In other words, it's a spirit of rebellion. And the enemy of our souls will play upon those two things....That's what the Antichrist will do. He's going to gain the kingdom by flattery."

By "flattery" Crismier means that politicians—and pastors—tell people what they want to hear.

"The Antichrist is going to come off as the greatest thing since sliced bread," Crismier said. "He's going to come in at a time when chaos is reigning supreme in the world....Nature abhors a vacuum, and he's going to...fill a vacuum that is actually being created intentionally right now through cancel culture....The American people, and people around the world, will have their cultures canceled so that they will no longer have any level of patriotism, or, shall we say, allegiance to their own country, to their own government, to their own people but are being prepared to enter into a whole new regime to unite the world in a one-world government...using a one-world religion."[6]

But what if this persecution is not related to the tribulation at all but is what Christians and Jews have commonly experienced at times throughout history? Many attempts have been made to snuff out Christianity, from the Roman persecution of the early church to the tumultuous Middle Ages to the days when our Puritan and Pilgrim forefathers sought religious freedom on foreign shores. Maybe what's needed now is not a road map to the future but a return to the steadfastness of our ancestors, who stood firm on the truth that no matter what happens, the Lord loves His children and promises to work all things together for good.

This aligns somewhat with an increasingly popular view among Christians, that the American church has perhaps had it too good and needs a dose of resistance to bring it back to its first love. People of this perspective say the church has grown lukewarm like the church in Laodicea—one of the seven churches mentioned in the Book of Revelation. This is our time to experience Chinese-communist-style persecution and share the Lord's suffering so we progress into greater maturity. Rather than take a posture of resistance, people of this view embrace the possibility of going underground and experiencing rejection, harsh treatment, imprisonment, and deprivation from mainstream American society.

It may be true that the church as a whole is lukewarm, but is grievous persecution the real answer to this? How does one go into such a future with any hope—or even plans?

One man who knows from experience is Pastor Andrew Brunson, who was imprisoned for his faith in Turkey for two years on trumped-up terrorism and spying charges before being released in October 2018. Brunson told CBN News that persecution and harassment toward Christ followers in America are about to intensify in many ways and that Christians should be ready for it.

"Jesus said that it would happen," Brunson said, "just as the world hated Him, that it will hate His followers."

Echoing Mike Bickle, Brunson expects "significant change in this area" because "many leaders in our society now—the corporate world, entertainment, media, politics, and also academia—do not honor God, and, in fact, they openly defy Him. They are increasingly hostile to those who identify clearly with Jesus and His teaching."

While persecution has started as a trickle, Brunson sees "a tidal wave on the horizon, and it's coming toward us very quickly. It's not some far-off threat."

What does this look like in an American context?

"One is in silencing, marginalizing, shaming, canceling people,"

Brunson said. "A big issue in the future for us is going to be communication, how we get our message out to other Christians, to non-believers also. What if you're banned from social media and no one will host your church website or your podcast?"

He also identified the danger of individuals or ministries losing their credit card processing providers or banks, which is already happening, as we have seen. Someday churches may lose their tax-exempt status for teaching biblical morality, and already some Christian teaching is being defined as hate speech.

"This is something that's really burning on my heart," Brunson said. "We need to prepare ahead of time so that when we are afraid (or under pressure), we do not run but stand firm."

He noted: "There are several ways to do this, but the number one that I want to underline is [this]: the way we prepare to stand in difficult times is by cultivating love for God....Over the years, this pursuit of God's heart prepared us for difficult assignments, including my time in prison. So God knew that I would struggle; He knew that I would break. But He also knew that because of all of those years of drawing close to His heart in the most difficult times, I would turn toward Him and not away.

"So the truth is that intimacy fuels perseverance, and we are willing to suffer for those we love," Brunson said. "The thing that best prepared me for my time under persecution was cultivating that love for God and running after His heart."[7]

A Call for a New Generation of Founding Fathers

There is clearly a purifying effect from persecution. Joel Kilpatrick calls cancel culture "a test of your susceptibility to mammon."

"Jesus said, 'You cannot serve both God and mammon,' typically translated as 'money,'" he told me, quoting Matthew 6:24. "There's a spirit behind this...fear of losing your job, of losing your reputation.... When the Lord turns up the heat and allows you to be persecuted or for your pocketbook to take a hit because you want to stand for truth,

He's putting you through a test. He's saying, 'Let Me see how much you're willing to stand with Me. Let Me see how much you love Me. What are you willing to put up with?'"

The thing that grieved Kilpatrick and many others during the outbreak of restriction and persecution in 2020 was seeing how many Christians are "motivated by mammon in the form of paychecks, retirement benefits, job benefits, security, keeping their house, keeping their kids in the school...or the university," he said. "Christians are wedded to mammon in so many different ways that all that the enemy has to do is put a little pressure on you, and you'll come to heel like a dog on a leash. That's behind a lot of the cowardice."

In his view if you haven't had money or opportunity taken from you because of your stand for Christ, then you have been failing some tests.

"The Lord brings us to places in life, each of us, where if we stand where He's standing, we're going to lose something," he said.

Kilpatrick recalled traveling to Ethiopia in the 1990s to report on the church there. He heard stories from pastors about how Ethiopian believers under the previous communist regime would gather in fields in the wilderness for days to hear the Word of God taught. They slept, ate, and worshipped in the fields—because they were so hungry for spiritual things.

"They didn't have...nonprofit protections and benefits that churches have here," Kilpatrick said. "Why do we need the benefits of a nonprofit to carry out the gospel effectively? Listen, if that's what's standing between you and powerfully preaching the gospel of the kingdom in your community, give up your rights under the government. Meet in a park or something."

He even questions whether churches need the degree of organization many of them have.

"The government can always use that...to control the church," he said. "We need to look past the normal structures...and start picturing a future where we're not going to subject ourselves to government control...through things like tax protection."

That said, Kilpatrick also believes persecution should call forth courageous leaders such as our Founding Fathers, men and women who boldly fight for liberty instead of meekly submitting to whatever the government does. Cancel culture, he believes, should summon people to action, not passivity—and Christians should be the first ones standing up to protect people's liberties.

"The improper reaction I see from a lot of Christians...[is], 'It looks like we're entering a season of persecution. We just need to hunker down and let the Lord refine us,'" he said. "I understand the suffering aspect of the faith....What I don't like is the passivity that it breeds. When people say, 'Well, look at the church in China; they have really flourished under these decades of persecution and the imprisonment...' But have you ever considered...if the church in China is doing so well, why haven't they overthrown the Chinese Communist Party yet? Why aren't they...giving any sort of pushback toward what their government is doing?"

Kilpatrick believes the Golden Rule and the second-greatest commandment ("Love your neighbor as yourself") both instruct us to protect our neighbors' God-given freedoms. This means not allowing the government to unjustly send your neighbor to prison, monitor people's behavior, or keep them from exercising freedoms of religion and speech.

"At some point, you [need a new generation of] George Washingtons and Thomas Jeffersons and Ben Franklins and Thomas Paines" to stand up in America and defend what makes our country godly and great, Kilpatrick said. "We need some Chinese people to stand up and be Founding Fathers there, because part of the Christian responsibility is to keep governments from stripping our fellow citizens of their God-given rights."[8]

Like Kilpatrick, I believe the genius of America is that we have preserved the rights God gives to every person: to live and speak freely, to train up our children with our beliefs, and so on. This has preserved His favor on our country for these 250 years because we have enshrined those protections in law. In Kilpatrick's view—and mine—those freedoms are worth fighting to preserve.

A Reinvigorated Mayflower Compact

One way of preserving God-given rights is by remembering and renewing our commitment to them. This happened in a profound—and perhaps prophetic—way in November 2020 for the four hundredth anniversary of the signing of the Mayflower Compact by our Pilgrim forebears.

A few weeks earlier Carter Conlon, former pastor (and now general overseer) of the famed Times Square Church in New York City, held a prayer event at a home on Lot One in Plymouth, Massachusetts, the site of the first house built by Pilgrims in America and likely where the fifty-one Pilgrims who survived the first winter prayed and covenanted with God for our land. I joined the event via livestream.

By the time the prayer meeting was taking place, the governor of Massachusetts had canceled all events scheduled to commemorate the landing of the Pilgrims in 1620 due to COVID-19.

Michele Bachmann, former Minnesota congresswoman and cochair of the Jerusalem Prayer Breakfast, attended Conlon's event. She and Jody Wood, a descendant of the Pilgrims and director of New York City Intercessors, decided they could not let this significant anniversary go unrecognized. In three short weeks the two women organized a private three-day event, including a three-hour global broadcast, from the first place where the Pilgrims met, prayed, and voted.

"This was highly significant because four hundred years earlier the Pilgrims gave humanity the governmental principle of 'rule by the consent of the governed,'" Bachmann told me. "We signed the original Mayflower Compact on board the re-created Mayflower, which sits in the harbor. We needed...to rededicate our nation and...reinvigorate the Mayflower Compact [for] today but also for the future" of the nation through "the next ten generations, should the Lord tarry."[9]

The two women invited Charismatic leaders to participate,

including Kevin Jessip, president of Global Strategic Alliance and cochair of The Return, a global prayer and repentance movement, and Jon Hamill, cofounder of Lamplighter Ministries, both Pilgrim descendants. The gathering highlighted the religious freedom on which our forefathers founded this nation.

I have a personal interest in the Pilgrims because my family has a historical connection to that era. I am a direct descendant on my mother's side of the family of William Brewster, a teacher and publisher who helped found the Plymouth Colony settlement and served as its senior elder and spiritual leader for many years. Through the Strang side of my family, I am also descended from the French Huguenots, who came to the New World in 1688 after some of the worst religious persecution in European history. As persecution rears its head in our day, I feel strengthened to stand because of the example of those brave family members from bygone eras.

Most Americans may not remember that the Mayflower Compact was the first document to establish self-government in the new world and was an early, successful attempt at democracy. It shaped the colonists' view of themselves and paved the way for future colonists to seek permanent independence from British rule. The inclusion of all the passengers as signers was one of the first expressions of a principle that would anchor the US Constitution: all men are created equal.

Hamill, a descendant of Richard Warren, one of the signers of the original Mayflower Compact, said it this way: "The move of the Holy Spirit was with them. In fact, when they wrote the Mayflower Compact…they said, 'in the presence of God, and one of another.'[10] They honored the presence of God, knowing that God had sent them apostolically across the waters to found a nation in freedom, to found a nation in covenant with Christ."[11]

It's obvious how low we have fallen culturally, morally, and politically in four hundred years, even as technology and knowledge advance at astounding rates. Yet Mike Bickle still sees what is unfolding today as part of God's plan as foretold in Psalm 2, a message that I mentioned earlier he first preached forty years ago, long before the growing persecution we now see in our nation.

"I'm not afraid....I'm alarmed. I'm alerted," he said. "I see the Lord smiling, going, 'You think this escalation is surprising Me and they get the last word? No...I have some plans that are going to knock the wind, in a good way, out of all of you. This thing is not over like you think it might be over. There's going to be My hand involved in a way that's going to cause My people to go forward in unity and with God's blessing on their lives.'"[12]

As darkness escalates and deepens, Bickle believes, a beautifully prepared bride will come forth, a great harvest of souls will come in, and the miraculous power of God will break out around the globe.

"God's not going to let our country go down," MyPillow's Mike Lindell told me. "We are one nation under God. The most important thing that everybody can do is pray."

Chapter 9

BEING THE CHURCH IN THE FACE OF CANCEL CULTURE

Twenty-two miles from California's Capitol building sits Destiny Christian Church in Rocklin, a church that for years has attracted around two thousand attendees each week and has been an encouraging place to hear the gospel and enjoy a sense of Christian community.

But founding pastor Greg Fairrington says he hardly recognizes himself, because since 2020 he and Destiny have been boldly standing against the governor's COVID-19 mandates and resisting efforts to muzzle congregations in the Golden State.

"In a way, [it's been] the most exciting time in my life...[and] ministry," Fairrington told me in a recent podcast. "That doesn't mean it wasn't challenging....Every week, we were believing and trusting at a level [that] maybe we have never believed in trusting God before....I would never trade the last year for anything in the world, even though [it has had] incredible challenges, incredible hardships....We leaned in to God like we had never leaned in to Him before."[1]

Eight weeks into the COVID-19 shutdown, Fairrington and his wife, Kathy, felt uneasy about keeping their church closed. They said to each other, "We have to open up the doors of this church; it doesn't seem right to us," Fairrington recalled.

They did it with a certain level of anxiety and trepidation because, like many people, they listened to the media and took for granted that the official narrative about the virus was fact. "The most difficult decision was to open the doors when the whole United States

137

said, 'You can't have church,'" Fairrington told me—but they felt called to do it anyway.

In preparation of defying the orders, they followed all typical protocols to a tee by holding four services instead of the usual two so the congregation could spread out, disinfecting the sanctuary between services, taking people's temperatures, and having them sign waivers and make reservations.

But Fairrington calls May 31, 2020, when they reopened the doors of the church, "a very traumatic day" because they were doing it essentially alone and with lingering uncertainty about what would happen. That morning, Fairrington stood on the platform for the first time since the church doors had been shut eleven weeks earlier and said, "Welcome home. Welcome to the house of God. Let's worship God."

"The place just erupted," he told me. "It was one of the highlights of my life."

So began a new era in the Fairringtons' lives, at Destiny church, and in the broader resistance movement of churches in California. Within weeks, as excitement built, many in the area gravitated to Destiny as a beacon of hope in a difficult time.

"As we got used to this thing, we became more comfortable. And more people were rallying around what we were doing, and we had to quickly expand and make changes," Fairrington told me. "The key words were *flexible* and *adaptable*. We had to make changes every single week of how we were going to accommodate people, because here's the sad truth...we were one of the only churches open in the area."

Running four services greatly taxed the staff, as did trying to maintain certain protocols, which eventually were dropped. Amazingly the church even offered children's ministries on the first day it reopened.

Of course, challenges arrived right on schedule. The church gained national media attention on Yahoo, CNN, and Fox News. But the local media was particularly "vicious," Fairrington said.

"The media was brutal on us," Fairrington told me. "The *Sacramento Bee*...did their best to cancel who we are; they have written, I think, twelve articles on us in a span of ten months. And they have taken me to task."[2]

That coverage included a negative article about the Fairringtons' daughter, who was married on New Year's Eve. The *Sacramento Bee* published an article essentially scolding the church for hosting the event,[3] and the local CBS affiliate sent a camera crew to the church to report on the "large crowds" that attended the wedding. Destiny church has been labeled "super-spreaders,"[4] and Fairrington was even dubbed "the death cult pastor" by one especially hostile group[5]—even though the church suffered no significant outbreak of the virus.

The media attention led to protests. Fairrington said that on two separate Sundays, a group associated with Black Lives Matter protested on the street where Destiny church is located, blocking traffic, shouting profanity through bullhorns, chasing families up and down the streets as they came to their cars, threatening churchgoers, and threatening the Fairrington family.

On one of the Sundays, Fairrington said, the protesting group decided to breach the lobby of the church while he was preaching. "We have a phenomenal safety team that created a human shield," he told me. "I was inside and didn't even know this was going on."

That morning, more than one hundred people gave their hearts to the Lord—even as the Rocklin Police Department was showing up in riot gear to move protesters off church property.[6]

But in northern California, that scene was all but unique.

Standing Alone

Like Rob McCoy in Thousand Oaks—whom Fairrington did not know at the time—Fairrington found himself isolated from other pastors because of his decision to defy the governor's stay-at-home orders. In anticipation of opening on May 31, Fairrington made phone calls to many pastors in his area, but not one would reopen with Destiny.

"Other pastors would not take a stand, [and] the strong people of their churches came to our church," he said. "Maybe [it was because some] were a divided house. They had either a board of directors [or] staff members who were not willing to take that step."

Fairrington can point to just one other pastor in the Sacramento area—Samuel Rodriguez of New Season church—who has stood and continues to stand with him.

"A whole lot of people thought we were losing our minds," Fairrington said. "That was one of the challenges; you would think you would be supported from people within the [Christian] family, people who are believers, or pastors or church leaders that we come alongside. They may not be taking the same steps, but you would feel like, 'Hey, I feel support there.' But it was a pretty lonely journey."

I asked Fairrington in a podcast to describe the state of the church in California, and his first response was that a "remnant church" is being birthed.

"They're bold. They're empowered by the Spirit of God. They are willing to say things that are deemed as hate in our culture, willing to take a stand, call sin, sin, deviant lifestyles, all that," he told me. "They know that this is the moment, and they're willing to put it all on the line. But it's not even close to being the majority; I would say that it's a very small minority."

I asked him why more churches didn't stand with him, if too many pastors are timid.

"*Timid* is a good word," he agreed. "Some people would say *cowardly*, but I've never used that word." People were afraid "of misinformation about the virus, afraid of the government and what would happen....I would get phone calls, like Nicodemus meeting Jesus, where nobody really would want to identify with me. [These pastors] would call me and say, 'Hey, can we have a private conversation?' The lead question 100 percent of the time was..., 'Can you give me a name of a good lawyer?' which tells me they were afraid...they would lose their church or get sued or whatever. So *timid* is a kind word."[7]

Joel Kilpatrick wrote an internet post early in the pandemic saying that emerging social pressures would act as a God-given flare to illuminate the battlefield.[8] The Lord, he said, was using COVID-19, racial strife, and the election to reveal people's hearts and minds.

Christians "were going to be coalescing on one side or the other," Kilpatrick told me. "Some [would say], 'Let's go along with everything the culture says to do, from COVID mandates to...leftist speech codes.'" Others—the resisting, freedom-supporting churches and people—would begin to coalesce and develop a bold, confident voice in the public square. At that point, there was little evidence of this happening and virtually no connection among pastors in California who wanted to peacefully but vocally defy public health mandates.

But pretty rapidly, "churches and leaders in the Christian world [began] to find each other...and gain strength and become a voice in the public square for the church of Jesus Christ," Kilpatrick said. "That was happening in California and nationwide, and it's going to continue."

Kilpatrick said, "Many leaders have shed their old skin...of being seeker friendly or just trying to be welcoming."

"There's nothing wrong with [being welcoming] in theory, but the way they were carrying it out was with a lot of compromise," he told me. "Some people today wouldn't recognize who they were a year ago because back then they just were meek and accommodating. Now they are warriors for the Lord and His kingdom and for the rights of not just Christians but all Americans. They stand up freely and say what they want without this fear of being canceled."[9]

Fairrington is certainly one of those who has undergone a profound transformation. After opening, he boldly confronted state leaders from his pulpit week after week. How did the governor and other civic leaders respond? With near silence. Fairrington said he received just one threat from a government official, who no longer is employed by the government. Indeed, Fairrington has tried repeatedly to meet with the governor and other leaders but to no avail.

"Our governor...would not even acknowledge the faith community," he told me. "We continue to ask, 'We would love to meet with you.' Nothing, zero, no response, not even acknowledgment of our existence."

There has been similar distance among numerous pastors in this religion-hostile state. Recently, Fairrington invited every pastor in the Sacramento region to join him at the state Capitol for a short press conference pertaining to a particularly disastrous bill concerning churches that was before the state legislature. Just five other pastors showed up, and nobody from the area's larger churches, aside from Destiny church.

"There's no unity," Fairrington said to me. "I don't know how it is in other places, [but] there's no unity in the state of California with churches—because we have people who have bought into the whole woke, CRT [critical race theory], Black Lives Matter…and it's not good. There's no unity here. Brothers are against brothers right now."[10]

David Lane of the American Renewal Project wrote recently that "disengagement from the culture by Christians left a void in America that is now being filled by everything anti-Christ" and that "the gathering storm engendered by baby boomers and passed on to the Millennial and Gen Z generations to sort out, will come down hard on the weak-kneed and lily-livered." I agree with that. Courageous people seem invigorated by challenges, while "avoiders" are terrified by them.

Quoting Christian minister and cultural theologian P. Andrew Sandlin, Lane dubbed our problem "Sunday go-to-meetin' Christianity" that makes no demands on the culture. It is a "self-effacing church culture, hidden behind the walls of the meeting place [and] not up to Christianity's required standards," Lane wrote. "A different type of Church will be needed for America to be born again. Budgets, buildings, and butts in seats won't be the theological focal point if America is to survive. Christians operating in the public square will be, empowered by wisdom from above."[11]

Mario Murillo, who was powerfully used in the Jesus movement of the 1960s and 1970s and speaks to millions via his blog, in-person revival meetings, and national television programs, says our generation needs Pattons to arise—referring to General George Patton, an American hero of World War II.

"[Patton's] fundamental approach to war in the natural is the precise tactic for war that we need now," Murillo told me. "For example, he didn't want his men digging foxholes." He was about "advancing, moving forward, taking the attack and the offensive to the enemy."[12]

Patton didn't care about public opinion because, as he said, "I've got a war to win."[13]

"Imagine if that spirit got on preachers today," Murillo said, "[if they were] not as concerned about public relations as [they are] about obeying God...and [preaching] sermons that please the Holy Spirit, even when they may offend other people."

Murillo labels this spirit "anointed resistance."

"Every minister...needs to ask themselves, 'Why am I in the ministry today? Am I a freedom fighter? Am I a resister? Am I going to allow my fear and need for self-preservation to take dominion over my duty as a leader?'" he told me. "I have told this to thousands of pastors in California: You are not violating the law by meeting in the church. They are violating the law by closing you down, because the Constitution says that no one will make a law in the United States to ban the free exercise of religion....They broke the law; you didn't. It's up to you to stand."

Every pastor, he said, is a freedom fighter now.

"It wasn't our choice, but it is now our duty," the veteran minister told me. "It wasn't perhaps what we went into ministry to be. But now that is what we are. And it is inescapable."[14]

Kingdom Engagement

Bethel Church in Redding, California, is known for celebrating a wide variety of political and cultural viewpoints within its community, though not unbiblical ones. Its entrepreneurial culture, saturated with prophetic encouragement, has spawned an extraordinary number of global ministries over the past couple of decades.

But when it came to recent legislation involving a basic moral issue in California, the church decided to publicly oppose it. I asked Pastor Bill Johnson about the approach he and the church take regarding influencing government toward right decisions.

"We have a responsibility before God....If you love people, and they're in the second story of a burning building, you've got to let them know....You can't make up excuses," Johnson told me. "We need to do it with grace and kindness and love, but loving people [means choosing] the best. And so it's a just mandate that we have from the Lord, to represent Him well with what He values."

The church at large, he said, is called "to give [people] adequate warnings and also instructions on how to do life. And that's what we've embraced as our assignment."

Much like my own family, the Johnson clan goes back at least five generations in the Pentecostal movement. Traditionally, Pentecostals have been reluctant to speak up about public issues, preferring to stick to things such as getting saved, filled with the Holy Spirit, and ready for the rapture. They prefer prayer meetings to political rallies.

"The Pentecostal movement, as you've acknowledged, has not been active on this [but] has been passive," Johnson said. "Part of the reason is, we actually have greater faith for the return of Christ than we do in the power of the gospel. And it's not either-or. We must have our anchor in the power of the gospel that is to change things now."

What does that change look like on the ground?

"It depends on who's in charge," Johnson told me. "Right now, with our present regime, I'm deeply, deeply concerned about the goals and ambitions of the far Left. I do think they're trying to work their way into the Bible being labeled as hate speech. I have felt that, though, for the last twenty years, that there was just slow progress toward that outcome.

"So several things," he continued. "The church has to get rid of this notion that we are not to be involved in politics. I do agree we're not supposed to be a political party; I get concerned with some of the expressions that I see from believers. But to be honest, I'd rather see excess on that level than no involvement at all.

"We've got to get rid of the notion that we just let things be as they are and the sovereign God will do what He wants to do. That's just really a foolish way to approach life, especially in a country where each individual citizen is given responsibility to choose and select. Our silence is a choice; it actually empowers the voice of those who are willing to stand up and to speak lies."

Some of the legislation before government leaders right now is "absolute insanity," Johnson said. "It would have been considered insanity ten years ago. Anytime you empower a five-year-old child to decide he's no longer a boy, he's a girl, and start giving him medical treatment, and the parents aren't involved—they have no authority, no power—that is absolutely unheard of that that would be considered reasonable. And yet we have people in leadership who think that's logical right now."

Churches, he said, must make our voices heard—but not through accusation, anger, resentment, or threats. "If you're going to drive an evil spirit out of a house, you've got to replace it with something good," he said.

Put adoption in place of abortion, for example, biblical identity in place of confused identity—solutions instead of problems.

"The Bible says that Jesus is the desire of the nations, which tells me everybody wants a King like Jesus; they just don't know it," Johnson said. "They love it when our family life works; they love it when business works. They love the creativity, the level of the outflow....We [as the people of God have] to present this in a way where people see that we're not just complaining against stuff, but we actually have solutions and answers that we'd like for them to consider."

While doing this, he calls on Christians to empower and support those serving in public office.

"Make room for them to serve, public service, as a spiritual assignment," he said. "It's as spiritual as any pastoral calling or calling for an evangelist or missionary....It's not to Christianize the nation; it's to bring the principles of the kingdom into play."[15]

A Voice From the Past

Without kingdom principles informing civic decisions, Francis Schaeffer, the respected Christian philosopher who died in 1984, warned decades ago that "you cannot build a stable system."

"What we're left with, in the humanist flow today in the United States, is purely variable, sociological law...a law that is merely based on what some group decides is good for society at a given moment," he said in his 1977 video series *How Should We Then Live.* "The Constitution of the United States today can be made to say almost anything on the basis of sociological variable law....The courts are actually making law. They're not only interpreting the law that the legislative has made, but they actually generate law....[This] arbitrary law dominates completely in communistic countries, but what most people don't realize is that...arbitrary law has swept over into the Western world as well."[16]

What is the alternative to "purely variable, sociological law"? For Schaeffer, it was nothing less than "a return to God's revelation in the Bible and as He has revealed Himself in Christ."

"When we accept Him as Lord, it means that we come to live under the...moral absolutes which the Bible gives, even if it sets us apart, as it did the early Christians from the surrounding culture," he said. "In this place, there are morals; there are values; there is meaning."[17]

Rick Joyner pointedly told me he believes the church is responsible for all our national problems.

The problems began with "the church abdicating its authority and responsibility in certain areas," Joyner said. "What we release in heaven or in the spiritual realm gets released on the earth, and it starts getting reflected in our government."[18]

Pastor Rob McCoy of Thousand Oaks, in a similarly barbed way, likes to ask pastors he speaks to how they are obeying Paul's admonition to Timothy to pray "for kings and for all who are in authority, that we may lead a quiet and peaceful life in all godliness and honesty" (1 Tim. 2:2).

"I say to them, 'Based on that pastoral epistle, could you name for me your five city council members and your five school board members that you pray for by name and the issues that they're dealing with in your community that would allow the citizens of your community to live quiet and peaceful lives in all godliness and reverence?'" McCoy said to me. "You can hear a pin drop. They don't know their council members; they don't know their school board members. We want our salvation to come on Air Force One. We want it easy; we want someone to do it for us, but to sit on a city council, you sit through five-hour meetings....It's hard work, and it's boring, and you don't get paid for it...or you get paid very little."

But teachers' unions and the like spend millions, if not billions, of dollars as the largest funder of political campaigns in California and other states to dominate local school boards—the same ones Christians don't want to participate in.

"While we've been busy doing church, the secular, progressive Left has dominated the *ekklesia*, [public square]," McCoy said. "We've been impressed with our buildings and our budgets and our baptisms and our homeless ministries, but we haven't participated in government."[19]

Many Christians believe that's not a bad thing. Their focus is on winning the culture through acts of compassion and service. But does it work?

Is Compassion Ministry Enough?

In contrast with those who occupy the political realm, some churches focus on doing what Jesus said to do: love others as we love ourselves by serving them during challenging times. We've often covered what some call "compassion ministries" in *Charisma* magazine. I believe this is a valid place to stand, but often churches that prioritize compassion ministry shun political affiliation or firm political commitment and believe Christians can win hearts and minds by doing acts of service.

Is it possible to forestall cancel culture—and even civil war—by emphasizing ministries of compassion and justice for the poor within the church? Is it possible to win our enemies with good works and overcome evil in this way? Or would this emphasis just make us dupes of a leftist state, the food pantries of an anti-Christian socialist regime? Is this strategy simply head-in-the-sand thinking? A reborn social gospel? A way of withdrawing from actual social and political engagement?

By keeping our mouths shut and feeding the poor, don't we end up being known by the same mocking epithet the communists used for people foolish enough to trust their goodwill—"useful idiots," at the service of an expanding anti-Christian state? And don't most Christian compassion organizations drift into spiritual ineffectiveness? Indeed, many, including some in the so-called evangelical world, have distanced themselves from the name of Jesus and biblical morality. Is majoring on compassion ministry a form of spiritual leadership or the white flag of surrender?

Many evangelical and Charismatic initiatives such as 1DayLA and Convoy of Hope are having an undeniably positive impact not just on cities but on nations. Their events can attract thousands and even tens of thousands of volunteers, fill stadiums, flood neighborhoods with good works, and provide free food and more for families in need.

The Dream Centers in cities such as Los Angeles and Phoenix do amazing work, and we could make a strong argument that they have changed parts of their cities (and states).

During the recent pandemic, fifty million people were suddenly classified as "food insecure,"[20] including families whose main bread-winners' income was cut in half, children whose only nutritious meals were those their schools supplied, and couples near retirement age who both lost their jobs. That prompted a major new initiative that included thousands of churches nationwide, the US Department of

Agriculture, and the White House Faith and Opportunity Initiative, led by Pastor Paula White-Cain.

Called Farmers to Families, it addressed a problem that arose in the wake of the pandemic: farmers' inability to sell their produce and other farm products to their regular outlets, such as restaurants, cruise ships, and hotels. With money from the large COVID relief bill, the USDA, with assistance from Ivanka Trump, developed a plan to purchase farm goods that would otherwise spoil and funnel them to needy families. But one piece seemed missing: local church involvement.

That's when Ivanka Trump told Dave Donaldson and Wendell Vinson, "The faith-based community is not involved in this program. But we realize if we're going to reach the last mile of need, we've got to engage the local church." Donaldson and Vinson, who leads Canyon Hills Assemblies of God church in Bakersfield, cofounded a local-church-focused compassion ministry called CityServe in Southern California in 2016. CityServe receives major food and non-food donations from large retailers and makes them available to churches of all sizes and denominations, enabling these churches to better serve people in their communities. Already, CityServe has developed an effective system of hubs and warehouse distribution centers in multiple locations.

"With [Ivanka Trump's] admonition and inspiration, we decided to create a faith-based collaboration for Farmers to Families," Donaldson told me. "Over fourteen million of these food boxes have been distributed through the local church to literally millions of people. And we call it also 'beyond the box,' where we've been able to pray literally with millions of people and hear their stories and how they've struggled through this pandemic."

These thirty-pound boxes of food contained dairy products, protein of some sort, and produce, and were distributed through local churches, Vinson told me. "The faith community in this time of crisis...leaned in," he said. "They said, 'We're going to serve, and we want to make a meaningful difference in our communities.' While many churches across the nation were shut down, they were serving, even though they couldn't gather in some parts of the country for services."

Donaldson told me that many churches have failed in the area of compassion ministry, which opens so many doors to the gospel. "Many of our churches have become weekend productions," Donaldson said. "They've lost their compassion muscle. Well, this is getting them back on the treadmill."[21] To help do this, his ministry recruits churches to be points of distribution and even launched an initiative at Grand Canyon University to equip students to help local churches.[22]

One of the many churches giving out Farmers to Family boxes is one I know well, City Church in Sanford, Florida, pastored by Eugene R. Smith, who founded the church twenty-two years ago. My wife and I have been members of City Church for the past several years, and we have seen the church live out its mission of "bringing God's love to the city...and leading people to become fully devoted followers of Christ."[23]

City Church jumped at the chance to participate in Farmers to Families. As lines of cars pulled into the church parking lot, volunteers not only delivered the boxes of groceries but also prayed for the people in the car line and invited them to church. Smith told me many of those who came for a box of food later attended the church and prayed to receive Christ.

But while the church reaches out to the community, some in the congregation feel it doesn't do enough. They criticize Smith for not jumping on the social justice bandwagon, and a few left the church because he refused to put the Black Lives Matter logo on the church website. To prove he was racially sensitive, Smith taught a six-week series on "racial reconciliation and our identity in Christ," with African American church leaders co-teaching with him every week. But even that didn't please everyone in the congregation. Then, when the church became a site where people could get the COVID-19 vaccine, others who feel the vaccine is unsafe or are afraid the government is going to require it, criticized him for that.

"We've become more tribal and divided than [at] any time in my life experience," Smith told me. "The sad reality is that it's become a distraction and a hindrance to our message and mission of proclaiming the gospel. To me that's sad. These are the people I see at church every week."

Meanwhile, Convoy of Hope, the huge humanitarian assistance ministry cofounded by my friend Hal Donaldson (brother of Dave Donaldson), distributed more than two hundred million meals in 2020. Convoy is well known for resourcing and mobilizing churches to serve their communities not only in the United States but around the world.

"The pandemic altered our delivery methods but did not prevent us from meeting needs," Hal Donaldson told me.[24] I found it interesting that during this season, they not only provided food but taught farmers and families how to grow food and even provided job training to women.[25]

Prayer Revival in an Open Church

Indeed, some ministries and churches emphasize compassion ministry and avoid political battles, but Christians are not called to forsake one in favor of the other. We are called to help those in need as Jesus instructed, even if that means being useful idiots at times. But we are also to stand firm against government overreach. Ministries embracing both callings are experiencing both political and spiritual revival.

Within months of Destiny church in Rocklin reopening to hold services, a full-blown prayer movement broke out, Fairrington told me, and church attendance swelled to five thousand people—double what it was less than a year earlier. Even more encouraging is the hunger for teaching about prayer—and civic engagement.

"Our Wednesday-night service…has exploded," he told me, adding that it sometimes draws two or three thousand people. "We felt the need to produce a civics class, and we had eight hundred people show up...in person and a thousand people online."

The strategic partnerships that Joel Kilpatrick foresaw are forming fast. Destiny welcomed state senator Shannon Grove to speak on a Sunday morning, and Fairrington said state assemblyman Kevin Kiley is a close friend and partner with the church in terms of supporting or opposing key legislation.

"We have a great relationship with them," Fairrington said of Grove and Kiley, adding that Kiley "has kept us as a church aware of what's going on. And we can call Kevin at any time." Fairrington also met and began teaming up with Rob McCoy, who is four hundred miles south of Sacramento, and other freedom-championing pastors.

"[There are] probably thirty of us who text each other on the same text thread," Fairrington said. "[It's] tremendous because we're all seeing it the same way. [There's] tremendous support there."

Destiny also started an initiative called Placer County Freedom to provide financial help to small businesses who were struggling because of California's severe response to COVID-19. "We have created partnerships in this community," he told me. "We have each other's back."

Unfortunately many churches around the nation seem to want to move backward rather than forward as things open back up. The recent Supreme Court decision blocking several states' rigid COVID-19 restrictions on churches has given many cover to resume doing what they did before.

Fairrington said his greatest fear in this moment is that the majority of churches in California are raising a banner that says, "We're getting back to normal." He added: "Because of the Supreme Court ruling... churches are now celebrating....They're actually doing a victory lap because the government told them it was OK [to return to church], not God....That just sends shockwaves up and down my spine."

I could feel his intensity as he continued.

"God forbid that we ever go back to normal!" Fairrington emphasized. "We can't go back to normal. Look what normal got us: the easy, fun church; church growth strategy; the spiritual amusement park that we all kind of bought into in the nineties and two thousands....It got us a weak church. COVID showed the weak underbelly of the church, not only in California but in our nation. And I pray to God we never go back to normal."[26]

Rather, he and many others want churches to be newly passionate about righteousness and the kingdom, willing to take bold risks to protect people and communities from government censorship and overreach.

I asked Doug Wead if Christians and churches should push back as hard as Fairrington and McCoy did and work to turn the tide—or is our cancellation inevitable?

"Yes, I think we should fight back, and I think we will be successful in fighting back," Wead said just as strongly. "That's the great lesson learned in history, that Christianity was crushed. The disciples died as martyrs. They were burned alive...in Nero's garden. But there were people fighting back; there were people creating safe houses. There was a network of Christians communicating with each other; the Scriptures were being created and written and copied, and there was great fight-back. It was the fight-back that created the modern civilization. Science owes its beginnings to those monasteries where scribes wrote and rewrote portions of the Bible....It's these heroes—these... mean little tough-spirited Christians who are fighting back—who will be the fathers of a new, tougher, stronger breed of Christianity."[27]

Chapter 10

HURRICANES OF REVIVAL

GOOD SPIRITUAL WINDS seem to be blowing again.

As a longtime Florida resident, I know a thing or two about strong winds and hurricanes. I've lived through a few. From June through November, weather conditions often cause a type of vacuum to form over the ocean. At these times, barometric pressure drops so deeply that it causes winds to rush in and equalize it—sometimes resulting in two-hundred-mile-per-hour gusts.

But what if this happened in spiritual terms to our nation? Mario Murillo believes it is about to. He doesn't mean winds of persecution or war—he means a hurricane of revival.

Murillo says the way hurricanes form paints a picture of what he sees happening in our society today. "One of the patterns for revival that Jesus referred to was weather," Murillo told me, referring to Matthew 24:29–31. "He said, 'You see the color of the sky and the cloud formations, and you know what's coming, and you don't discern the signs of the times.'"

Murillo said the big flashing sign of the times today is spiritual hunger and a vacuum of answers. When there is a vacuum of good, something must rush in to fill it. Observing the cultural signs, Murillo believes it is "inevitable that the revival is coming."

"The natural hunger for God is something that no atheist can abolish, no university can ban," he said. "No human engineering is ever going to be capable of erasing man's deep desire to know God and the inner emptiness that they feel....When you create a culture where you don't know what gender you are, you don't know what love is, you don't know what's up, what's down, what's truth, what's false, who you can believe—all of a sudden, these deep, eternal yearnings rise to the surface, and people turn to God."

Murillo believes the spiritual vacancy and hunger are profound in our day, much like a hurricane, and "when God's Spirit falls on a culture that is starved for truth, it will overrun the walls of the church." We have seen this happen many times through history in the great revivals we now honor and celebrate.

"The hunger is there," Murillo said. "The tide of spiritual awareness has gone out so far that the youth are starved....It could be a new Jesus movement; it could be something else. But anyone who supposes that something big is not at work is going to miss it."[1]

Heaven's Library

Murillo became well known in Christian circles during the Jesus movement in California in the 1970s as a fiery young evangelist who saw young drug addicts, social radicals, and many others come to Christ.

More than a generation later, other young leaders are rising up to also declare the approach of a coming revival. One such person is a young pastor named Chris Reed, a relatively new voice on the national scene whose gift of highly accurate and timely words of knowledge has already had a huge impact on leading ministries in America.

Reed told me that at the end of 2020 he had a spiritual encounter in what he calls the "library" of heaven with an angel he said was named The Fear of the Lord. What the angel said has a lot to do with the revival many believe is about to sweep the globe. I felt it was important to include it in this chapter.

In this encounter, Reed felt a holy reverence and awe as he was drawn to a bookcase labeled "The Supernatural" and to a specific book there titled *The Seven Spirits of God*. On the front cover were the words "The Spirit of the Lord." Each page, he told me, was thick and white, like a book within itself. The first page was titled "The

Spirit of Wisdom"; the next, "The Spirit of Living Understanding or Revelation"; the third, "The Spirit of Counsel"; the fourth, "The Spirit of Might"; and the sixth, "The Spirit of Knowledge." These correspond to the description of the seven Spirits of God listed in Isaiah 11:2.

Reed turned the book over, and the back cover read "The Spirit of the Fear of the Lord." He glanced up and then down to see that the back cover had been torn off, and then all the pages in the book fell out. He was left holding the front cover, which read "The Spirit of the Lord."

The angel with him in this library said, "Do you understand what you're seeing? What you are seeing is the result of when the fear of the Lord is torn out or is missing in the church. You lose the Spirit of counsel and might....You lose the Spirit of wisdom in everyday situations, knowing how to apply knowledge and wisdom....You lose the Spirit of revelation, [so people] operate out of intellect and head knowledge."

Finally, he said, "When you lose the fear of the Lord, all you're left with is an atmosphere." Reed instantly thought of the many church services he had been in where he didn't see the Spirit of might in the form of miracles, or the Spirit of knowledge in words of knowledge or revelation, but people still said, "We feel the Spirit of the Lord. We feel the presence of the Lord."

"There's got to be more than just an atmosphere and...a feeling that the Spirit brings," Reed told me. "We've got to have the full, complete Spirit of God at work, or all we're left with is an atmosphere."

The full work of the Spirit comes when the fear of the Lord is present, he said. That means a reverential awe and a hatred of all kinds of sin, according to Proverbs 8:13, which says, "The fear of the LORD is to hate evil; pride and arrogance and the evil way and the perverse mouth I hate."

"Holiness, godliness returns to the church naturally when there is a sovereign outpouring of the Spirit of the fear of the Lord," Reed said. But it doesn't end there. Reed drew my attention to Acts 5, where we read about Ananias and Sapphira, who fell dead after they lied about their giving. The result was that "great fear came on the entire church and on all those who heard these things" (v. 11).

This immediately led to the return of signs and wonders at an unprecedented level, a supernatural unity, a heightened respect of the church by the world, exponential growth, a harvest of souls, angelic activity, and the healing of the sick in unprecedented ways. All these results are found in Acts 5 after the fear of the Lord returned to the early church.

So much is tied to "a restoration of the fear of the Lord," Reed told me. "There is a complete, sevenfold, perfected element of the Spirit of God at work in the church again. That's what we want."[2]

The Kindness and Severity of God

We badly need the fear of the Lord because, as renowned pastor and theologian Dr. R. T. Kendall believes, "America is under judgment."

Kendall's recent book, *We've Never Been This Way Before*, details this judgment and why it's happening through the biblical lens of Joshua leading the people of Israel into the Promised Land. "God is fed up, and He is angry," Kendall said. He sees four reasons for the judgment on America: "racism, legalized abortions, same-sex marriage, and theological liberalism in the pulpits."

But Kendall also sees hope. "God is at the bottom of it, but it's gracious judgment," he said. "It means that He's trying to get our attention. It's not retributive judgment, where God just gets even and punishes. No, He's been gracious to us to get our attention, to drive us to our knees, and it will end up with America crying out like they've never done before.

"God will answer," Kendall said. "And it's my view the only thing that will save us will be this awakening, not unlike what we saw in the eighteenth century under the preaching of people like Jonathan Edwards or the Cane Ridge Revival in the early nineteenth century. We're talking about something huge, not ordinary revival—something that gets the attention of the world."

Kendall shared a brief story from Joshua 5 to point out a critical need in our nation. "As Joshua entered into the Promised Land, he saw this awesome figure. Joshua said, 'Are you for us, or for our adversaries?' And the figure, which happened to be an angel, [said], 'Neither.'

"Well, that was not the answer Joshua wanted," Kendall said. "What we need to learn about God—and what has been forgotten—is that He is a God of glory, and He does things for His own glory. Jonathan Edwards, who is the main figure in the Great Awakening of the eighteenth century, used to say the one thing that the devil cannot duplicate…in us is a love for the glory of God. The flesh cannot produce it; only God can do it.

"Joshua was learning that we do not have any entitlement," Kendall said. "The curse of our generation, in my opinion, is a feeling of entitlement. The idea is that we can snap our fingers and expect God to jump. There is no fear of God in the world today; there's no fear of God in the nation. There is little, if any, fear of God in the church, and that will be restored. And that is what the angel was saying to Joshua. And I think what we need to learn and what is going to bring about this great awakening is a restoration of the fear of God. That's my conviction. That is the need of the hour."[3]

What Is This Coming Revival?

Hundreds of leaders for dozens of years have spoken of a reality they call "the next great awakening," "the greatest revival in history," and other superlatives. What exactly are contemporary leaders saying about this coming move of God, and are they simply echoing one another and perhaps speaking fond hopes rather than future realities?

One prominent voice in this chorus belongs to Sean Feucht, whom you may have read about in *Charisma* or whose viral videos you may have seen online. He is an on-fire preacher and worship leader who has brought the presence of God to Christians in many parts of the world. After the COVID-19 outbreak in 2020, Feucht began holding outdoor worship concerts in various parts of the country. When others were feeding on fear, Feucht and his growing group of followers went hard after God. Feucht is no slouch in the public arena either—he ran for Congress, albeit unsuccessfully, in northern California in 2020.

In August 2020 Feucht shifted his focus to leading Let Us Worship, a series of outdoor revivals he has been holding across the country. You can tell something's working when the legacy media attacks it and starts throwing around hackneyed insults such as "super-spreader." *Rolling Stone* blared that slur in a headline that asked, "Jesus Christ, Superspreader?"[4] Feucht embraced it and had T-shirts emblazoned with the slogan, but of course he means a super-spreader of the gospel of the kingdom.

Many who attend his events have already come to know Christ, but the fact that they show up by the thousands virtually everywhere Feucht goes to lead an evening of worship demonstrates their deep desire for spiritual things. Yet Feucht has received withering criticism from within the ranks of Christians too, especially from young people who fault him as being insensitive, even dangerous, because of his actions during the pandemic. The comments on his social media at times resemble knock-down, drag-out arguments between those who think he's spreading love and freedom and those who think he should "obey governing authorities" and respect the decisions of those in political power.

Headlines have declared Feucht is leading a new Jesus movement,[5] but what do his events really tell us, that the revival is already upon us, or that the hunger for revival is here but the actual awakening hasn't arrived just yet? The most optimistic view, and the one I take, is that God is answering the prayer for more laborers in the harvest. The young people who show up are willing to brave scorn and even physical threats, like the ones worshippers faced during Feucht's event in Seattle.[6] This shows a level of mettle that will be necessary should the world react violently against the coming move of God.

Rather than trying to determine what his events are pointing to, perhaps we should ask instead, What would life be like if Feucht weren't out there holding these worship events? Who or what would have filled that gap? The many thousands who follow his events on social media or attend them in person receive powerful encouragement. He has raised a Christian standard in a difficult season in a way few people have been brave enough to attempt. Clearly, God is using him to bring forth an army that He will deploy for His good purposes.

The Church Must Wake Up and Expose Corruption

Various faith leaders with divergent ministries have echoed Feucht's call for the church to arise. Mario Murillo isn't a politician, nor does he pretend to be one. He has spent much of his life traveling the globe to share the gospel of Christ. But back in 2012 the Lord told him to begin a blog about political issues, and he obeyed.

That blog, at mariomurilloministries.wordpress.com, has now had more than 12.5 million readers, and God continues to use Murillo to speak unvarnished truth to today's believers. More than ever in this postelection season, Murillo says, the church must expose the corruption and allow God to take us beyond what he calls a "Red Sea moment" and into the promised land of last-days intimacy with Him.

"I'm telling people right now that the church is divided against itself," Murillo said in a recent interview. "One of the reasons that I believe the church was in worse shape before the pandemic than now is because we had no idea how wimpy and divided and disconnected from reality the church was. Many, many leaders wanted a big church; they were willing to make some costly mistakes in order to change from reforming a culture to having a large empire."

Murillo said the concept of cheap grace has led to the church's lack of engagement with the governmental mountain of influence. "We had no political involvement because we didn't sense danger," he said. "And sensing danger was something that didn't go with the image of the new God the Father, who was so into us that He had compromised every one of His attributes in order to appeal to us. So we had no heart for war.

"Here we are right now....We're at the Red Sea. And some Christians are saying, 'Well, let's just side with Biden and let this go. Let's not investigate.' We're looking bad to the world because they don't have a clue what's at stake. They're saying, 'Oh, well, you know, in four years, Trump could run again.' Well, right now we're having the weasel guard the chicken coop. And the fact is, we don't know what we're going to look like in four years—if there'll be anything for Trump to save."

The church's laissez-faire attitude is at fault, but God has promised protection for the righteous, Murillo said. "Jesus said to the Laodicean church, 'You believe you don't need anything.' We had years of that; we had years of becoming experts in marketing, planning, multi-campusing, all this stuff. But we did not preach the counsel of God to America. So therefore, in Revelation 3, God said, 'You're poor, miserable, blind, and naked, and you don't know it.' Then He said, 'I stand at the door and knock.'"

That's what everyone must listen for—"that knock," Murillo said. "...This is the paradox of the hour. God is affording us an intimacy with Him that has not been available to prior generations. God is saying, 'Just as they are delving into dramatic evil and wickedness, you can enjoy intimacy and righteousness with God, and a peace that passes understanding.' But not if we don't open the door. We [must] open the door, and He will come in. And all of these tremendous blessings of the last days will be unfolded."[7]

Jane Hamon, known initially as the daughter-in-law of apostle Bill Hamon of Christian International in Florida, has now received acclaim for her own powerful prophetic ministry. She offered her interpretation of God's purposes in this unique season.

"I think God's wanting to keep us focused in prayer," Hamon told me. "God's wanting to keep us focused in believing the Lord but then trusting the prophetic words that have come through so many different prophets during this last season of time through dreams and visions and all kinds of ways. I believe that we would be remiss if we just threw up our hands and said, 'Well, that's that.'"

She believes we're in a place to do as 1 Timothy instructs and "war a warfare with the prophecies that have gone before us. And so that's our responsibility," Hamon said. "It's God's responsibility for the outcome, but it's our responsibility to align with what the prophets have said—to pray, to decree, and to war against the forces of darkness and…corruption that I think would like to rob from this nation the destiny and purpose that God has called us to."

Despite the current chaos, Hamon believes the church is already moving into a season of revival. She says this revival will look different from the Toronto Blessing or the Brownsville Revival of years past, and this awakening will take place largely outside the church.

Hamon said God told her, "An awakening is an epidemic of revival, or pandemic." In other words, today you "catch" revival, "then everybody you get around catches it, and everybody they get around catches it," she said. "I don't believe we're in a COVID crisis or any kind of economic [growth] crisis; I believe we're in a spiritual crisis for the heart of a nation….It's going to be a widespread, massive move of God, but it's got to start with every single one of us."

Hamon also has words of encouragement for the church as it grapples with the unprecedented challenges of our day. "God has a plan in the midst of all the chaos that's going on," she said. "He warned us at the beginning of [2020] and said, 'Listen, this is going to be a year that you're going to have to overcome some things.' That's the only way you become an overcomer, is to overcome some things. You're going to have to stay focused on what Jesus has spoken to each individual; each person is going to have to get focused on that. And we're going to have to get very optimistic about the promises of God, that His promises are for revival and awakening; His promises are for a mighty comeback."

The church in America, she believes, is rising, waking up, and "being set on fire by the anointing of the Holy Spirit. The enemy's come in to try to bring a lot of discouragement and a lot of despair. And I really believe that it's time for people to shake themselves and wake themselves and recognize that we're coming into the church's greatest hour....I believe that God is going to use the United States to preach the gospel to the ends of the earth again, and I believe that God is waking up believers out of their slumber and bringing them into a full expression of the destiny, the purpose, the calling of God."[8]

Listening to (and Weighing) Prophecy

I have long believed in prophecy. Growing up in a Pentecostal denomination, I was taught that New Testament prophecy is for today. Even so, it wasn't until the Charismatic movement in the sixties and seventies that people in the church widely began to recognize prophets, but the role of prophet remains controversial in many circles.

Some of the harshest critics dismiss prophecy, saying that any prophet who "gets it wrong" should be held to Old Testament standards for false prophets. Others insist that the gifts of the Spirit—including the gift of prophecy—ended when the last apostle died. This has become the major differentiation among Protestant Christians, who would generally agree on other New Testament doctrines such as the existence of the Trinity, the importance of the Lord's Supper, the necessity of personal salvation, and the need to have faith in God and focus on prayer.

Yet the apostle Paul, who wrote more than one-fourth of the New Testament, said, "We know in part, and we prophesy in part" (1 Cor. 13:9). The Modern English Version says to "examine" all prophecy (other translations say to test it), implying a prophet could miss the truth (1 Thess. 5:21). I've seen so-called prophets get it wrong, such as Edgar Whisenant, an engineer and Bible teacher who wrote *88 Reasons Why the Rapture Will Be in 1988*. I know one local Christian station that apparently raised a lot of money because its viewers were so excited about that book. Other "prophets" on the fringes of Pentecostalism have focused on "personal prophecy" and even supplied these prophecies to people who gave large offerings for a personal "word from God." But this is not to say leaders with prophetic insight (who do not charge and actually hear from God) cannot give accurate prophetic words.

Over the years, I've received prophecies that were stunningly correct. The late Paul Cain called me out of a service in 1990 and gave me a public prophecy about seeing me as a fourteen-year-old looking through Venetian blinds at a lake and land and even said the number 722. He also said God has had a calling on my life since that relatively young age.

I was stunned. When I was fourteen, I lived at 722 Venetian Avenue in Lakeland, Florida. No one but immediate family would have known that detail—certainly not Paul Cain.

Another personal prophecy, by Marilyn Hickey in the 1970s, when *Charisma* was struggling to survive financially, encouraged my wife and me because she said God had His hand on our little magazine. She loved to quote from Isaiah 6:3, which says, "The whole earth is full of His glory." She loved to give scriptures as prophecy and was saying that in its own way, this fledgling magazine would fill the earth with God's glory.

For that reason and many others, my ears are open when proven prophetic voices such as Rick Joyner, Lou Engle, Bob Jones, John Paul Jackson, and many other godly people say God has shown them that a massive move of the Holy Spirit is on the way. My heart yearns for it to happen again in America.

Harvest of Justice

My longtime friend Ché Ahn, senior pastor of Harvest Rock Church in Pasadena, California, and apostle of Harvest International Ministry, a global network of over twenty-five thousand affiliated churches and ministries, since the 1980s has been praying for and preaching about the need for revival to come afresh to America. Little did he know that part of his assignment would be political.

Unlike McCoy and others, Ahn was never politically active until the State of California and the City of Pasadena came down hard on him for not remaining closed for months on end in 2020. Ahn and the church rose to an even greater national prominence when his church filed a lawsuit against California governor Gavin Newsom, whose extensive mandates even tried to limit and shut down home Bible studies and prayer meetings, all under the guise of public health.[9] Ahn's case spent months bouncing from court to court.

During that time, the State of California threatened him, his staff, and church members with a year's jail sentence for his refusal to stop holding services, as well as a $1,000 fine for each violation of the governor's order. If upheld, the amount would have been massive. Threats of imprisonment came, Ahn said, and the fines reached into the millions of dollars. While his friends and family were concerned for his safety and well-being, the longtime pastor and apostolic figure remained unmoved. He knew the case would create a breakthrough not only for his church but for every church in California. After months of legal battles, the Supreme Court decided to hear Ahn's case and ruled in his favor six to three.

"Thank God for President Trump nominating and confirming three conservative judges," Ahn exclaimed to a room full of applause at one of his pastors' events in Florida in March. "I've been to over a hundred nations worldwide, and I'm standing before you today to testify that even with all of our issues and all of our problems, America is still the best nation in the world by far!"

As we reported on Charisma News, the major political victory has only fueled Ahn's hunger for the great revival he and many others see on the horizon. He has been traveling the country, calling Christians, and especially Christian leaders, to seek revival and repent while also standing firm to resist unjust, slavish governmental policies, such as the ones his court case helped strike down.

Following the results of the 2020 presidential election, Ahn said God drew him to a place where he was even more desperate to hear His voice for this moment in history. He cried out to God and felt a fresh filling of the Holy Spirit come upon him as well as an anointing to step into the ongoing struggle for the soul of our nation.

With a renewed touch from heaven and a fresh commissioning from God, Ahn received what he called a "spiritual download" regarding where the church in America goes from here. God showed him what he calls the "blueprint of historical revival" and told him to call the church to action. In a recent address to pastors, Ahn proclaimed three points of this blueprint:

1. **The church gets revived.** Scripture tells us that judgment begins in the house of God (1 Pet. 4:17). Many in the American church have dumbed down the requirements of the gospel in order to be relevant to our culture, Ahn said. Yet in our newfound "cultural relevancy," we have become irrelevant to the kingdom of God moving on the earth. As a result, many pastors and leaders are bound by spirits of fear and of pleasing man. "Even though it is now legal to meet in California, churches are paralyzed with fear, and many won't have in-person services," he said.

2. **The harvest comes in.** This doesn't refer to a soul getting saved here and there but rather to a moment of time when the masses are turning to Jesus. Ahn referenced the mighty Welsh Revival that occurred in the early twentieth century and the more contemporary Jesus movement, which took place from 1967 to 1977. Some twenty million people found Christ as their Lord and Savior during the Jesus movement, reports estimate.

3. **Society is transformed.** Genuine historic revival must include the transformation of society—the salvation of souls on the micro level and the renewal of government systems on the macro level, Ahn said. He referenced the English politician William Wilberforce (1759–1833),

who worked tirelessly over decades to see the slave trade abolished in Great Britain. Ahn proclaimed that abortion is the chief scourge of our nation today and as long as we have life in us, we must work to protect the lives of the unborn.[10]

Strategy for Revival and Reformation

Ahn said he's "tired of playing games and playing church." He told the group of pastors that "we must get serious about seeing our nation changed."

Now is the time for revival and societal transformation, said Ahn, who has been sharing a strategy for revival and reformation with pastors across the nation. Ahn said when God gave him the strategy, he put a fleece before the Lord, as Gideon did in Judges 6:40, and invited twelve megachurch leaders to a meeting to discuss what he heard God tell him. If all twelve came, he would know his strategy to mobilize the church of America came from God. What was the strategy?

1. **Establish a house of prayer in every church to contend for revival in California and the United States.** Pray specifically for the government and governmental leaders. Prayer moves the hand of God, and it is our privilege and responsibility to come before the throne of grace to implore God's mercies over our communities, he said.

2. **Equip and encourage fivefold leaders to return to and maintain their first love for Jesus.** Every local church pastor must resist the temptation to let their love grow cold because of the lawlessness now being unleashed in our country. Now more than ever, pastors and leaders must press in to God and rekindle their first love for Jesus and the gospel.

3. **Activate local churches in personal evangelism, and partner with Ephesians 4:11 evangelists in public revival meetings.** California churches are partnering with ministers such as Mario Murillo, Sean Feucht, and Jay Koopman to gather the lost and share the gospel en masse. Ahn said it's time to once again "cast our nets" to reach a harvest as never before.

4. **Plant as many *ekklesias*—small groups in the marketplace, homes, or churches—as possible.** Ahn has a vision for small groups forming across the nation where believers work together to stay focused on the gospel and on letting God use them for the purposes of revival and reformation in every sphere of influence.

5. **Activate every believer to be involved in the government mountain by exercising their privilege to vote biblically and also to run for local, state, or national office.** From city councils to school boards, there are vacancies that should be filled with godly, Bible-believing people with hearts to serve God and serve their communities. Changing and impacting our government must be practical, and if every local church has at least one person elected to office, we would immediately see a massive impact on the societal and political climate in America.

Not only did all twelve of those national leaders attend Ahn's meeting, thereby confirming the word the Lord gave him, but at the end of that meeting, he asked every one of them to commit to seeing this vision fulfilled and to sow a seed of $10,000 each to start funding the mission to which God was calling them. Each leader made a financial commitment, and since then, Ahn hasn't looked back.

"I love this nation, and I want to see transformation like never before," Ahn told the gathering of pastors. "Remember the prophet

Haggai, who said, 'The glory of the latter house will be greater than the former.'"

After Ahn spoke, a tangible sense of faith and excitement filled the room. Pastors stood to receive a fresh impartation from the Lord to go to their churches and implement what was spoken of, with many carrying a fresh energy and vision for the days ahead.

Ahn then encouraged the pastors by recalling a testimony he heard from Mario Murillo. Before Murillo hosts a crusade in a city, he invites local pastors to gather to hear about plans for the event. Murillo typically has 100 to 150 pastors attend such events. But recently he sent out an invitation for the first evangelistic crusade he conducted since the 2020 election. The response was overwhelming and unprecedented, with first a hundred pastors signing up, then two hundred. The two hundred grew to five hundred and kept rising until the ministry had to cap the event at a thousand pastors registered to gather with hopes of seeing a revival in their city.

God only knows what will happen next. But all signs point to the fact that the rumblings of revival are beginning. Every church, pastor, and believer will have to decide how to participate in God's purposes in the earth at this time. Let us pray that God will indeed send a fresh revival to our land and that it does nothing but grow in intensity and spiritual fervor that we might see a mighty awakening in our day.[11]

Loosed From Lukewarmness

Chris Reed has been spending time with leaders in the prayer and prophetic movements and sees a widespread return to an intentional life of prayer and fasting.

"The grace for this hour is to deliver the church of the Laodicean spirit mentioned in Revelation 3...this lethargic, apathetic approach that is a result...of a lacking of the fear of the Lord," Reed told me. "Through difficulty, through persecution, a church is arising in this hour, a remnant within the church that I believe...will be delivered from that Laodicean spirit."

But returning to our first love for Jesus doesn't mean taking it on the chin from cancel culture, in his view.

"If there's ever a time in history where we need bold, brave, and courageous Christians and leaders, it's now," Reed said. "This is no time for weakness....We need soldiers of the cross that are not willing to back down in the face of the enemies of the cross."[12]

In Ken Fish's view, a revived church will save civilization itself. "If we will follow the ways of God, we will find that in general, He will bless us and will increase us," Fish told me.

He also pointed out the sometimes overlooked effect of awakenings and sincere spirituality on society. Fish referenced a book by Max Weber called *The Protestant Ethic and the Spirit of Capitalism*, which examines how nations that put biblical principles into practice experienced greater prosperity in Europe. Weber wrote that northern European countries (which embraced what's become called the "Protestant work ethic") prospered more than the southern European countries.[13]

"That's why we hear more about economic crisis, central bank problems, currency devaluations, [and] inability to service debt... [in] southern European countries than we do in [northern European nations]," Fish told me. "It all goes right back to this idea that they were...trying to embody and to live out the values and the teachings that are found in the Scriptures....It is not a perfect one-to-one correspondence, but the trend line is indisputable."

He said that over a couple of hundred years, this trend produces a phenomenon that has been noted by missiologists as "redemption" and "lift."

"Those who follow the ways of God find redemption, and they are lifted out of their oppression and despair to higher levels of economic prosperity," Fish told me. "This is a better way to live because God's vision ultimately is that every man [and woman] should sit under his own vine and fig tree; I'm quoting...the Hebrew prophets. God wants us to be able to control our own economic destiny under Him, not unto ourselves, but underneath His guidance....All of this is tied together in the American experiment, and it's part of what has made us the most prosperous and successful nation on earth."[14]

Contrast this with the Soviet Union, which went so far as to punish overachievers in a factory line. As I conducted research for this book, historian Doug Wead pointed out this sad fact to me. "You couldn't lag behind, or you'd be punished. But if you excelled and did better than everyone else, you were manifesting outrageous and improper egotistical tendencies. So you had to be gray, down in the middle somewhere," Wead told me.

My point goes beyond financial prosperity to things of even greater value in society: dignity, mutual value, and a sense of humanity toward one another.

Wead tied the Western idea of equality of people to the Christian concept of the Good Shepherd who leaves the ninety-nine and goes out to save the one that is lost. "That is the antithesis of Communism," Wead added. "In Communism, everything revolves around the ninety-nine; the one can die. But the ninety-nine must be saved and preserved, and it's the will of the commune. So that's where we're headed, in my humble opinion, and the cancel culture's a manifestation of that process."[15]

Philosopher Francis Schaeffer pointed out in the seventies that "when people believed indeed that man was made in God's image, there was a real basis for humanness. I'm saying humanness, for people being human. But once this is removed, as it has been now so largely removed for the loss of the Christian consensus, there is no reason—once we see people merely as a machine, as not qualitatively different from non-people, non-man—there's no reason why we should not tinker with them...genetically. And there's no reason we shouldn't manipulate them. And there is no reason why we shouldn't control them....That's exactly where the humanist ideals take us."[16]

Meanwhile, Wead finds the positive in all of this. "The good news is that Christianity can't be stopped. If it could have been stopped,

Karl Marx would have done it. They tried to kill them all....They punished people for being Christians, and it just came right back like mushrooms growing up in the grass after a rainstorm....The fact is, while they were burning Christians alive in Nero's gardens, Christians were whispering to each other in the catacombs beneath Rome, 'Maranatha'"—their code word meaning, "Come, Lord," or more positively, "Our Lord is coming."[17]

"Christianity has survived the hatred of government and its enemies before, and it will survive this too," Wead said.[18]

If cancel culture and pressure from all sides have served to awaken the church in America, then we can truly see that God uses all things for the good of those who love Him. If there is a correspondence between difficulty and triumph, then we may be in for something truly historic in the near future. Call it awakening; call it a hurricane of revival.

Just be sure to pray for it to come.

Conclusion

ALL THINGS WORK TOGETHER FOR GOOD

Tony Perkins, who is the head of the Family Research Council, the former president of the Council for National Policy, and one of the most visible and principled evangelical voices in the nation's capital, recently posted a Bible study video in which he pointed out that the prophet Jeremiah had faced cancel culture in his day for revealing a conspiracy.

"What was the conspiracy?" Perkins asked. "They willfully, with intent, were doing just what their fathers had done...to undermine the authority of God and to trade the truth for a lie."

When Jeremiah revealed this conspiracy, God called the people to account, telling them, "You're saying on the surface that you're listening to Me, that 'in God we trust,' but in reality, you are not trusting in Me. You are not obeying Me." The men of Jeremiah's own town, those closest to him, came against him to silence him.

Cancel culture, in Jeremiah's day and in our day, loves "the darkness, and they do not want their deeds to be made known," Perkins said. But Jeremiah knew he had to speak the truth.

"As believers we must speak the truth. That's what God has called us to do," Perkins said. "The cancel culture will come against you, but they will not prevail against you. [The Lord says], 'You will accomplish the mission I have sent you to accomplish.'" Yes, "the cancel culture is real, and they will fight against the light of God's Word. Just make sure that what we are saying is the Word of God. It's not our opinions, not our thoughts, but rather what the Word of God says."[1]

There has been too much teaching in Charismatic circles, and even non-Charismatic evangelical circles, that the sign of God's blessing is a smooth life with good health, good income, and perfect marriages and families. That was not Jeremiah's experience—or that of the disciples or any other believers in history. We were born into a battle. Today, that battle is against things like cancel culture and communism, among many other manifestations of darkness. We can't ignore these things; I am convinced that we must confront them lovingly but without backing down or watering down the truth.

We can be thankful that voices of freedom are speaking out more and more and joining together for greater strength. One evidence of this is the Philadelphia Statement, which now has more than thirty thousand signatories. (The entire statement is in appendix B.) This well-argued, relatively short declaration reads in part:

> Social Media mobs. Cancel culture. Campus speech policing. These are all part of life in today's America. Freedom of expression is in crisis. Truly open discourse—the debates, exchange of ideas, and arguments on which the health and flourishing of a democratic republic crucially depend—is increasingly rare. Ideologues demonize opponents to block debates on important issues and to silence people with whom they disagree.
>
> ...The American tradition of freedom of expression, complete with its attendant responsibilities, is our school for democratic citizenship....Tragically, we are losing these defining features of our democracy. Common decency and free speech are being dismantled through the stigmatizing practice of blacklisting ideological opponents, which has taken on the conspicuous form of "hate" labeling. Responsible organizations are castigated as "hate groups." Honest people of good faith are branded "hate agents." Even mainstream ideas are marginalized as "hate speech." This threatens our ability to listen, discuss, debate, and grow.
>
> ...If we seek to change our country's trajectory; if we desire unity rather than division; if we want a political life that is productive and inspiring; if we aspire to be a society that is pluralistic and free, one in which we can forge our own paths and

live according to our own consciences, then we must renounce ideological blacklisting and recommit ourselves to steadfastly defending freedom of speech and passionately promoting robust civil discourse.[2]

I agree with those eloquent, principled words, and in this book I have gone further to identify the deeper roots of cancel culture and how it affects Christians in particular. Perhaps believers need a unifying statement of our own—a Declaration of the Rights of Christian Citizens, to borrow a Jeffersonian title from a different revolution. These rights certainly include the right to speak clearly and without fear about political and social issues from an openly Christian, biblical point of view. The fact that we must argue for this at this point in our history shows just how much freedom we have already lost.

A "Ten Times Change" Season

George Orwell is sometimes credited with saying, "In a time of universal deceit, telling the truth is a revolutionary act."[3] Mario Murillo told me he often receives criticism for being so outspoken about "woke culture." Some Christians want to know why he doesn't just preach against sin or try to get drug addicts free, as he was known to do as director of Resurrection City in Berkeley, California, back in the hippie era.

"When I used to preach against drugs, everybody loved me. And when I preached against gang violence, everybody loved me," Murillo said. "But then when socialism became the worst drug in the ghetto, and the Democratic Party became the most dangerous gang in the ghetto, it was a natural evolution to start talking about those things."

The church and its leaders are in a time of what he dubs "Ten-x change," meaning a change exponentially larger than most. He likens it to when a big-box store moves into town, throwing every local hardware store into instant crisis. The situation forces small business owners to rethink their future and repurpose themselves for survival and success.

"When wokeness struck America...we didn't realize all the subterranean tentacles that it had in so many institutions," Murillo said.

Believers will only weather and thrive in this sudden—or sudden-feeling—change if they allow God to retool them and their message for the times we live in.

"We can't be afraid of how different we're going to look if we obey God in a woke and cancel culture, because His approach and the message to this culture is going to be different," Murillo said. "There are fresh words that God wants to use and fresh tactics He wants to anoint."

He recalls seeing Chuck Smith take his small Calvary Chapel church in a direction that seemed radically different compared with status quo churches of the 1960s and 1970s. While other churches refused to welcome hippies who wouldn't wear shoes—or men who wore long hair—Smith welcomed these sometimes unsightly but spiritually hungry young people. As a result, Calvary Chapel defined a new, highly attractive approach to doing church that helped transform a generation.

"That same context is here now," Murillo said. "The church needs to go back to God, surrender before God, get fresh fire in the glory of God, and see what the natural tactics and priorities that emerge from that revolution are and [those] that will be perfect for the times we're in."

A major aspect of this emerging approach involves a return of signs and wonders to the church. Murillo points out, rightly, that the church is not automatically respected as it was in the days when Billy Graham was considered "America's pastor" and most businesses were closed on Sundays.

People no longer defer to the church, he said to me. "They're willing to shut us down...and openly mock us. We need a fresh verification of our right to tell people to repent. That isn't going to be in the spurious, [emotional] meetings but in the kinds of meetings that...Oral Roberts and Kathryn Kuhlman had, with medically verified miracles followed by a balanced presentation of the Word of God....Today, the issue of…national repentance will be strengthened by the presence of…miracles of God in our meetings."

That won't remove the need to turn people away from harmful lifestyles and beliefs.

"In order for the church to survive, it's not that they have to get political," Murillo said. "It's more a matter of depoliticizing the evil, saying, 'I'm not against you because you're a Democrat but because of the evil that you're doing to the nation.' We need to identify it; we need to speak against it."[4]

I agree, so I chose his words to help conclude this book. The subject of cancel culture is not some faddish ideology we can expect to vanish on its own. Rather, many Americans, and especially Christians, can see that our rights are being taken away. We are experiencing cancellation, and many of us can see for the first time that we are dealing with communism in the country we have always believed was the land of the free and the home of the brave.

My question—and the one suggested by this book's title—is, Where is God in all this? I believe in an omniscient, omnipotent God. None of this caught Him by surprise. He has plans and purposes greater than anything we can understand. He knows the beginning from the end. Scripture lets us know there will be hard times before the end of the age. There will be the rise of a strong leader who promises to bring peace. The Book of 1 John calls him the Antichrist. There will be terrible wars culminating in the Battle of Armageddon. But ultimately Jesus triumphs and ushers in a millennium of peace, during which every knee shall bow and every tongue confess that Jesus is Lord. I remember Bob Mumford saying in the seventies, "I've read the back of the book, and we win."

Is this simplistic thinking? Nonbelievers may say it is. Many don't believe it and would rather mock what the Bible says. But we know God's Word is true—all of it, no matter what the haters and would-be cancelers of Christianity say. As I and others in these pages have pointed out, there have been many attempts to stamp out Christianity, and these attempts have always failed. They will fail this time too.

Jesus Himself said no man knows the day or hour of His return. It's looking more and more as if it will be anytime, and it seems to be drawing near at warp speed. But a great awakening may change the direction of world events. Life was challenging and the church corrupt in Martin Luther's day. Yet the Reformation changed everything and affects our lives even today. No matter what, we must be faithful. None of us asked to be born in this generation. But God looked down through time and preordained what is happening. He put us here for a purpose.

One scripture that comforts me is, "All things work together for good for those who love God, to those who are called according to His purposes" (Rom. 8:28). When I decided to write about current events and how Christians should respond, I originally wanted to call the book *All Things Work Together for Good*. I even researched if that title had been taken. (It hadn't.) The words of that verse struck me because despite what we are seeing, they are still true. If we believe God's Word, we must believe that promise, even if things look worse in the natural with each passing day.

My main concern continues to be that Christians will retreat, become silent, and self-censor, going along with the tide of events. If we're despondent and fatalistic and do nothing, then those wanting to cancel our godly heritage and outlaw biblical values win. Remember what Edmund Burke is credited with saying: "The only thing necessary for the triumph of evil is for good men [and women] to do nothing."[5] The words remain true today. As Pastor Rob McCoy reminded us in chapter 7, there are more of us than there are of them.

Is it possible that good will come of the cancel culture trend? Of course. I even see it beginning now. Many Christians who were previously complacent are more passionate for God than ever. We see the glimmers of a great revival. Would that happen if everything were just peace and prosperity, as Francis Schaeffer said? I don't think so. Americans are waking up and speaking up—and the cultural bullies and government overlords are beginning to notice.

I've tried to make these points and show not only how bad things are (and they could become even worse) but also what's being done and what needs to be done. I've talked with leaders who are making a difference and offering insights and strategy. But it's not just their battle—it's yours and mine too. None of us can afford to be a mere spectator. Each of us has a part. I believe God had a purpose in you reading this book. If you've read this far, I know you're engaged and looking for answers. May they come through prayer, observation, conversations, and participation in the great causes of our day.

I encourage you to stand up, speak up, and push back at the cancel culture bullies before it's too late. But don't just target the secular, godless bullies; call out complacency and sin in the church. As I wrote earlier, the problems in society accelerated because the church has not been the church for the past several generations. The problems we face are not new. They aren't just the result of social media fact-checkers or socialists winning political office. They go deeper than that.

While we can't change the past, each of us has a role in changing the future. It starts with changing ourselves—confessing our own passivity and sin. Training our children in the right way to live. Influencing our congregations and communities. Getting involved in government, media, academia, and the other mountains of influence in our society. And praying and believing God to work a miracle and to send revival and save America, not judge it.

Whether or not things change overnight—or change differently than we expect—we can rest assured that God has a plan and that indeed "all things work together for good."

EPILOGUE

THE STORMS OF cancel culture continue. Just before this book went to press, the Jerusalem Prayer Team, whose mission is "to pray for the peace of Jerusalem," was deplatformed by Facebook right after fighting flared up between Palestinians and Israel.[1] The Jerusalem Prayer Team Facebook page, with a reported seventy-seven million followers, was taken down when Facebook was bombarded with messages from several hundred thousand anti-Israel radicals who didn't approve of the Jerusalem Prayer Team's support of the Jewish state.

As a longtime journalist who has made my living for decades as an editor, I try to avoid redundancy. But I want to end with a call to action by repeating—or reemphasizing—some important thoughts sprinkled throughout this book. I share them again as encouragement and exhortation to take action on what you've read.

In chapter 8 missionary Andrew Brunson, who suffered for two years in a Turkish prison before President Donald Trump intervened in 2018, told us American Christians to be prepared for persecution. This means more than just stockpiling food or arming for violence. We must be prepared not to become offended at God for allowing such things to happen. This view of suffering goes against a lot of Pentecostal-Charismatic teaching that God is a good God who lovingly protects His children from anything bad. Actually, I believe that. I also believe suffering is part of life. I believe both are true in the same way I believe Christ is all God and all man.

A mature believer knows the Christian walk involves dealing with seeming contradictions. Jesus Himself said, "In the world you will have tribulation. But be of good cheer. I have overcome the world"

(John 16:33). In a recent podcast, Brunson told me he almost turned his back on God in prison but didn't because earlier in his life he had developed a real intimacy with the Lord. He said: "The thing that best prepared me for my time under persecution was cultivating that love for God and running after His heart."[2]

Let me end with practical ways you can respond to what may be ahead. I was encouraged to do so by my close friend Evan Trinkle, a retired US Army colonel who made thoughtful suggestions after reading an early draft of this book.

"Encourage your readers to be vocal," he told me. "Now is not the time to be passive or think someone else will warn others. Tell them to pass out copies of the book. Also, get involved in community, state, and national issues. Don't be timid to call local, state, and federal officials."

He continued: "Ask what is their standard for making decisions. If it is the Bible, dig in and find the answers to the tough questions of life people are wrestling with right now. Allow God to use you more in the everyday matters of life. You can, if willing, influence the culture around you. Speak up about the cancel culture; don't participate in supporting businesses that cancel your voice."

Finally, he suggested: "Pray for God's intervention. Pray for a great move of God upon the United States of America and around the world."

This parallels advice given in chapter 6 by the late John Paul Jackson, who offered six ways to weather the coming storms, which warrants repeating:

1. Don't overreact to media hype and spin.

2. Simplify and streamline your life.

3. Reconnect with friends and family.

4. Rethink your focus.

5. Be an influence in the culture.

6. Take more time to listen in prayer.

Jackson was a longtime friend who tragically succumbed to cancer in 2015 at age sixty-four. I love how he relayed something the Lord told him: "Little battles produce little victories and result in little champions. Great battles produce great victories and result in great champions. Which do you want to be?"[3]

By engaging in "great battles," we are being obedient Christians who are occupying until He comes, as Luke 19:13 instructs us to do, no matter what shape, size, or scope cancel culture and persecution take. We are made to be great champions winning great victories. These days are ours!

Appendix A

A BOLD MESSAGE FOR AMERICA

Delivered by Rabbi Jonathan Cahn, January 25, 2021

THIS IS JONATHAN Cahn. Two hundred and thirty-two years ago, in the first-ever presidential inauguration, the nation's first president addressed a jubilant multitude and a nation that was united in shared values and a common hope in America's future. In that first-ever presidential address, George Washington gave the newborn nation a prophetic warning. He said this: "The propitious smiles of heaven cannot be expected on a nation that disregards the eternal rules of order and right that heaven itself has ordained."

In other words, if America followed the ways of God, His eternal rules of order and right, the blessings of God would remain upon it. But if America should ever depart from the ways of God, then His blessings would be removed from the land. And now January 20, 2021, another presidential inauguration takes place, and the nation's capital city, named after that first president, has become a military zone. For the first time in American history, a presidential inauguration is devoid of people.

Instead of a jubilant crowd, twenty-five thousand American troops stand guard over the National Mall, in which flags stand in for the missing people and barbed wire surrounds the halls of American government. There is no war; there is no overt threat from beyond its borders. Rather, the threat comes from within. Division infects the land, as does a plague that has kept its citizens masked and locked in their houses as the nation's functioning has been, in large part, paralyzed.

For months, America's cities have seen protests and riots and doors and windows shuttered and buildings set on fire, and the nation's most revered edifice of government, the Capitol Building, taken over by an angry mob, with the nation's leaders fleeing for safety.

And so the prophetic warning that was given on that day of that first inauguration: the smiles of heaven are being removed from the land. And so the question must be asked: Have we then disregarded the eternal rules of order and right that heaven has ordained? America, as did ancient Israel at the height of its prosperity, has turned away from God. We've driven Him out of our public squares, out of the schools of our children, out of our culture, out of our lives, and as did ancient Israel, in place of His absence we've let in other gods and serve them. We've rejected His ways and embraced the ways of immorality. We've called evil, good, and good, evil. And as did ancient Israel, we've lifted up the most innocent among us, our babies, and shed their blood. Israel sacrificed thousands of its children; we've sacrificed millions, tens of millions [of] unborn children, who are not here this day, this inaugural day, because we took their lives.

And their silent screams ascend to heaven, and their blood is on our hands. We pass down rulings from Washington, DC, that war against the eternal laws of heaven, on human life, human nature, gender, marriage. We've indoctrinated our children against the ways of God. We have done as we were warned not to do, and then we wonder why the blessings of heaven are being removed from our land.

When judgment came to ancient Israel, it manifested in the form of an enemy attack, a strike on the land, a wake-up call. It came to America on September 11, 2001. And it came to the very place where George Washington stood and prayed on the day of America's first presidential inauguration. The biblical template of national judgment then ordains a period of years in which the nation is given the chance to return to God or else head to judgment. In the case of ancient Jerusalem, that period, from that first enemy strike to the year when the greater shakings began, was nineteen years. From the strike on

American soil in 2001 to the nineteenth year brings us to the year 2020: the year when the great shakings began.

The danger that this window of time is drawing to an end is now upon us. We stand in a most critical moment. Mr. President, President Biden, you have called for unity and peace. But how can a nation have unity and peace when it wars against the very foundation on which it stands? How can a nation have unity and peace when it has turned against the God who brought it into existence?

And it has turned. The nation that once led its schoolchildren in prayer and taught them of His Word now declares such prayers and teachings to be forbidden and now instructs its children against the ways of God. How can that nation have unity and peace? How can we have unity and peace in America if we have no unity and peace with God? We are a house divided against itself, and a house divided against itself cannot stand.

Mr. President, how can you place your left hand on the Bible, the Word of God, and then with your right hand sign laws into existence that war against His Word? How can you place one hand on the Word that ordains human life as sacred, and in the image of God from conception, and then with the other hand sign laws into existence that will promulgate the killing of that human life, of those children? How can you invoke the name of God in your oath and lay your hand upon His Word and then implement laws that will suppress the going forth of His Word, that will censor His Word and those who advance it? You plan to enact laws that will disregard the distinction between male and female, men and women. Did not the warning of our first president involve that very thing if we disregard the eternal rules of order that heaven itself has ordained.

You plan to enact laws that will specifically neutralize the protection of religious freedom. You plan to strike down the Hyde Amendment so that more children will be murdered, and those Americans who recognize abortion as murder will be forced to support the act of murder with their taxes. And you plan to empower the act of killing unborn children not only within the borders of America but throughout the world, to the end that yet more rivers of blood will flow. How does one do such things and name oneself as a believer in God and a follower of Jesus? How does one sign the sign of the cross and then sign decrees that rage against what God has so clearly set forth in His Word concerning life and death, holiness and sin, righteousness and immorality, good and evil? To you, Mr. President, and all who have joined you in this agenda, from the vice president to the leaders of the Senate and the House, and all who sit in halls of power and have embraced this agenda, heed this warning.

This day will pass. The applause of men will fade. This administration will inevitably be over. This world will pass away, but you will stand before God and give account. For it's written in His Word that we will each stand before God and give account. And on that day all the power you once wielded will be gone, and all of the world's approval and praises will have faded away, and all the fame and glory you received will amount to nothing. In the day when the book of history is closed, and the Book of Life is opened, none of that will matter. It will be you and Him. And you will be required to give account of what you have done. Did you follow the will and Word of God, or did you not? If you pursue these things, then you did not, and the blood of children will be on your hands. And then will come eternal life—or eternal judgment.

The voice of God calls out to you and to all to turn and follow Him with all your heart, who gave all His heart and life that you might be saved. As for America, the problem is not social or economic or cultural or political. The problem is ultimately spiritual, and so must be the answer. America has turned away from God. And its only hope is that it return to God. Choose true greatness and lead in that return or continue in this departure from God to destruction and judgment.

As for those of you who love this nation and are burdened and fearful for its future, America's only hope is revival. Return. Without it, the nation is lost. And revival only comes through repentance and return.

It's time to pray as never before that return and revival would come. But it's time not only to pray for revival, but to choose revival, to choose to live in revival now. And for that we must each commit to return to God, to put away from our lives that which must be put away and take up that which must be taken up and walk in His ways and live in His Spirit, as we have never done before. "For the eyes of the Lord search to and fro throughout the entire earth, looking for the one whose heart is completely His to show Himself mighty on their behalf." Let us be that people, and revival will come.

And if the darkness must come, whether by persecution, or disorder, or disintegration or apostasy, do not fear, for God is still on the throne, and the darkness cannot overcome the light, but only magnify it. And if the darkness should grow darker, then it's time for the lights of God to shine even brighter, for it is no longer the time of the candle in the day. It is now time for the candle in the night. We are now the candle in the night that shines against the darkness and lights up the night, the world, with its radiance. We pray that the civilization that was established and consecrated to be a city on a hill, America, would once again shine with a light that once illumined it.

But whether or not it does, it is time that each of us shine with a light of His glory. It is time to live unhindered, uncompromised, unbound, bold and all-out on fire and mighty in the power of the living God. For thus says the Lord: Arise and shine, for your light has come and the glory of the Lord has risen upon you. Deep darkness shall cover the earth, but the glory of God shall rise upon you, in the name above every name that is named, the name of Yeshua HaMashiach, Jesus, the Messiah, the way, the truth and the life, the King above all kings, the Lord of all, the hope of the ages and the answer to every life, the star of Jacob, the prince of life, the glory of Israel, the Lion of the tribe of Judah, the name that will remain above all names when all is passed away, Yeshua, Jesus, the same yesterday, today and forever, Amen.[1]

Appendix B

THE PHILADELPHIA STATEMENT

I SIGNED THE FOLLOWING statement, known as the Philadelphia Statement, and I encourage you to do so also. You can find it at https://thephillystatement.org/.

Social Media mobs. Cancel culture. Campus speech policing. These are all part of life in today's America. Freedom of expression is in crisis. Truly open discourse—the debates, exchange of ideas, and arguments on which the health and flourishing of a democratic republic crucially depend—is increasingly rare. Ideologues demonize opponents to block debates on important issues and to silence people with whom they disagree.

We must ask ourselves: Is this the country we want? Surely not. We want—and to be true to ourselves we *need*—to be a nation in which we and our fellow citizens of many different faiths, philosophies, and persuasions can speak their minds and honor their deepest convictions without fear of punishment and retaliation.

If we seek a brighter future, we must relearn a fundamental truth: Our liberty and our happiness depend upon the maintenance of a public culture in which freedom and civility coexist—where people can disagree robustly, even fiercely, yet treat each other as human beings—and, indeed, as fellow citizens—not mortal enemies. "Liberty is meaningless where the right to utter one's thoughts and opinions has ceased to exist," Frederick Douglass declared in 1860. Indeed, our liberal democracy is rooted in and dependent upon the shared understanding that all people have inherent dignity and worth, and that they must be treated accordingly.

A society that lacks comity and allows people to be shamed or intimidated into self-censorship of their ideas and considered judgments will not survive for long. As Americans, we desire a flourishing, open marketplace of ideas, knowing that it is the fairest and most effective way to separate falsehood from truth. Accordingly, dissenting and unpopular voices—be they of the left or the right—must be afforded the opportunity to be heard. They have often guided our society toward more just positions, which is why Frederick Douglass said freedom of speech is the "great moral renovator of society and government."

The American tradition of freedom of expression, complete with its attendant responsibilities, is our school for democratic citizenship. It trains us to think critically, to defend our ideas, and, at the same time, to be considerate of others whose creeds and convictions differ from our own. It enables us to learn from, and peacefully live with, one another despite differences. It further instills in us an understanding that the mere exposure to ideas we find offensive is not an act of "violence." And it admonishes us that if we value the freedom of expression, we must extend the same measure of freedom to others, even to those whom we believe have gone very wrong in their thinking.

Tragically, we are losing these defining features of our democracy. Common decency and free speech are being dismantled through the stigmatizing practice of blacklisting ideological opponents, which has taken on the conspicuous form of "hate" labeling. Responsible organizations are castigated as "hate groups." Honest people of good faith are branded "hate agents." Even mainstream ideas are marginalized as "hate speech." This threatens our ability to listen, discuss, debate, and grow.

Blacklisting is spreading. Corporations are enacting "hate-speech" policies to protect people from "wrong" and "harmful" content. Similarly, colleges and universities are imposing speech regulations to make students "safe," not from physical harm, but from challenges to campus orthodoxy. These policies and regulations assume that we as citizens are unable to think for ourselves and to make independent judgments. Instead of teaching us to engage, they foster conformism ("groupthink") and train us to respond to intellectual challenges with one or another form of censorship.

Humanity has repeatedly tried expunging undesirable beliefs and ideas. What self-appointed speech arbiters, whether in the majority or in the minority, fail to grasp is that they will likely eventually become the targets. The winds inevitably shift, sometimes rapidly. The question is whether civility norms and free-speech safeguards will remain in place to protect them, or whether they will become victims of the dangerous precedents they themselves have established and advanced.

To be sure, our free speech tradition is not absolutist. It does not embrace certain, limited categories of speech, such as defamation, obscenity, intimidation and threats, and incitement to violence. Yet the idea of "hate speech" exceptions to free speech principles is foreign to our free speech ideals, impossible to define, and often used by those wielding political, economic, or cultural power to silence dissenting voices. That is why we must favor openness, to allow ideas and beliefs the chance to be assessed on their own merits; and we must be willing to trust that bad ideas will be corrected not through censorship but through better arguments.

If we seek to change our country's trajectory; if we desire unity rather than division; if we want a political life that is productive and inspiring; if we aspire to be a society that is pluralistic and free, one in which we can forge our own paths and live according to our own consciences, then we must renounce ideological blacklisting and recommit ourselves to steadfastly defending freedom of speech and passionately promoting robust civil discourse.[1]

ACKNOWLEDGMENTS

I N MY PREVIOUS book *God, Trump and the 2020 Election*, I acknowledged every source and every person who helped with the book. I doubt everyone I thanked even read it. In hindsight it may have been overkill, so this time I am going for brevity. My deepest gratitude goes to my:

- **Writing team**: Joel Kilpatrick of Westlake Village (Thousand Oaks), California, who helped craft the book you are reading, and Marti Pieper of Seneca, South Carolina, who is a better wordsmith than I'll ever be. I enjoyed working with this team!

- **Editing team**. In our Charisma Media headquarters in Lake Mary, Florida, I want to thank Debbie Marrie, Melissa Bogdany, and the others in the book group—especially Adrienne Gaines, my primary editor.

- **Administrative team**. I'm grateful to my wonderful wife, Joy, co-owner of Charisma Media and its chief financial officer, who has been very supportive but told me I could not extend my deadline because our company needed the book to release during the fall book-selling season! My secretary, Chris Schimbeno, was also a huge help in handling a myriad of details and tasks. Also, I appreciate the executive team I work with every day: Joy Strang, Dr. Steve Greene, and Ken Peckett.

I also want to thank several friends who encouraged me and more importantly prayed for me during the writing project. Finally, I want to thank the Holy Spirit for the inspiration to write this book and the Lord Jesus Christ for ultimately canceling the curse of sin—the cause of everything wrong with the world, including cancel culture.

ABOUT THE AUTHOR

STEPHEN E. STRANG has served the Pentecostal-Charismatic movement since the 1970s when he founded *Charisma* magazine at the age of twenty-four. The magazine's motto—"encouraging you to experience the power of the Holy Spirit"—is also his life message. Trained as a journalist at the University of Florida, he worked for several years at the *Sentinel Star* (now the *Orlando Sentinel*) before being led to start *Charisma* in 1975.

For more than four decades he has looked for new ways to serve those who believe in the power of the Holy Spirit. In addition to publishing magazines and books (seventeen of which have made the *New York Times* best-sellers list, the best known being *The Harbinger* by Rabbi Jonathan Cahn), the company he founded, Charisma Media, has published books in Spanish, a line of children's curriculum, and even the Modern English Version of the Bible.

Today, Charisma Media is one of the world's leading Pentecostal-Charismatic publishing houses. As technology has changed the publishing industry, the company has launched many digital products, including the Charisma Podcast Network, which in mid-2021 had sixty-five million downloads, and an audio version of *Charisma*. Its newest venture is Charisma PLUS, an OTT platform to communicate "the power of the Holy Spirit" in a new way to a new generation.

God and Cancel Culture is Strang's seventh book. His recent books have been featured in nearly all Christian media outlets as well as on Fox News, MSNBC, and CNN. Over the years, he has interviewed four US presidents and won many journalism awards, and in 2005 he was named by *Time* magazine as one of the twenty-five most influential Evangelicals in America.

Strang is married to Joy Strang, who is co-owner of Charisma Media and its chief financial officer. They have two grown sons, Cameron and Chandler, and one grandson, Cohen.

To see Strang's books or to subscribe to *Charisma*, go to www. stevestrangbooks.com. Listen to his *Strang Report* podcast on the Charisma Podcast Network.

NOTES

Introduction

1. "Elon Musk's Neuralink shows monkey with brain-chip playing videogame by thinking," Reuters, April 9, 2021, https://www.reuters.com/technology/elon-musks-neuralink-shows-monkey-with-brain-chip-playing-videogame-by-thinking-2021-04-09/.
2. *Amazing Grace*, directed by Michael Apted (Los Angeles, CA: Samuel Goldwyn Films, 2007).
3. History.com Editors, "Slavery in America," History.com, accessed May 5, 2021, https://www.history.com/topics/black-history/slavery.
4. Eric Metaxas, *Amazing Grace: William Wilberforce and the Heroic Campaign to End Slavery* (New York: HarperCollins, 2007), 85, 96–97, https://www.google.com/books/edition/Amazing_Grace/NtDXPcC-7WAC?hl=en&gbpv=0.
5. "William Wilberforce (1759–1833): The Politician," The Abolition Project, accessed May 5, 2021, http://abolition.e2bn.org/people_24.html.
6. Michael Ray, "Tea Party Movement," *Encyclopedia Britannica*, updated December 6, 2020, https://www.britannica.com/topic/Tea-Party-movement.

Chapter 1

1. Doug Wead, "Doug Wead Says Christianity Is 'First Thing They Want to Silence,'" April 15, 2021, in *Strang Report*, podcast, https://strangreport.libsyn.com/interview-with-doug-wead.
2. Wead, "Doug Wead Says Christianity Is 'First Thing They Want to Silence.'"
3. Petr Svab, "Communist Tactics to Force Self-Censorship Sweeping America," *Epoch Times*, updated March 11, 2021, https://www.theepochtimes.com/communist-tactics-to-force-self-censorship-sweep-america_3724784.html. Used with permission.
4. Svab, "Communist Tactics to Force Self-Censorship Sweeping America."
5. Catie Edmondson and Michael Crowley, "Hawley Answers Trump's Call for Election Challenge," *New York Times*, updated

January 15, 2021, https://www.nytimes.com/2020/12/30/us/politics/josh-hawley-trump-election-challenge.html.

6. Wead, "Doug Wead Says Christianity Is 'First Thing They Want to Silence.'"

7. Svab, "Communist Tactics to Force Self-Censorship Sweeping America."

8. Joel Kilpatrick, "The Cancel Culture With Joel Kilpatrick," March 9, 2021, in *Strang Report*, podcast, https://www.charismapodcastnetwork.com/show/strangreport/3c927297-7064-4316-93a7-b05a0b32313d/The-Cancel-Culture-with-Joel-Kilpatrick.

9. Mark Pratt, "6 Dr. Seuss Books Won't Be Published for Racist Images," AP News, March 2, 2021, https://apnews.com/article/dr-seuss-books-racist-images-d8ed18335c03319d72f443594c174513.

10. "Statement From Dr. Seuss Enterprises," Dr. Seuss Enterprises, March 2, 2021, https://www.seussville.com/statement-from-dr-seuss-enterprises/.

11. Pratt, "6 Dr. Seuss Books Won't Be Published for Racist Images."

12. Barack Obama, "Presidential Proclamation—Read Across America Day, 2016," The White House, March 2, 2016, https://obamawhitehouse.archives.gov/the-press-office/2016/03/01/presidential-proclamation-read-across-america-day-2016.

13. Pratt, "6 Dr. Seuss Books Won't Be Published for Racist Images."

14. Abigail Shrier, "Gender Activists Are Trying to Cancel My Book. Why Is Silicon Valley Helping Them?," Quillette, November 7, 2020, https://quillette.com/2020/11/07/gender-activists-are-trying-to-cancel-my-book-why-is-silicon-valley-helping-them/.

15. Shrier, "Gender Activists Are Trying to Cancel My Book. Why Is Silicon Valley Helping Them?"

16. Abigail Shrier, "Does the ACLU Want to Ban My Book?" *Wall Street Journal*, November 15, 2020, https://www.wsj.com/articles/does-the-aclu-want-to-ban-my-book-11605475898?mod=searchresults_pos8&page=1.

17. Target initially reinstated the book but then removed it again; Shrier said no explanation was given. Madeline Osburn, "Target Swiftly Bans Book on Behalf of Anonymous Twitter User Crying 'Transphobia,'" The Federalist, November 13, 2020, https://thefederalist.com/2020/11/13/target-swiftly-bans-book-on-behalf-of-anonymous-twitter-user-crying-transphobia/; Tré Goins-Phillips,

"All Over Again: Target Removes Abigail Shrier's Book Critical of Transgender Agenda," Faithwire, February 24, 2021, https://www1.cbn.com/cbnnews/2021/february/all-over-again-target-removes-abigail-shrier-rsquo-s-book-critical-of-transgender-agenda.

18. Grace Lavery (@graceelavery), "...steal Abigail Shrier's book and burn it on a pyre," Twitter, November 14, 2020, 5:41 p.m., https://twitter.com/graceelavery/status/1327743402289623042.

19. Glenn Greenwald, "The Ongoing Death of Free Speech: Prominent ACLU Lawyer Cheers Suppression of a New Book," Glenn Greenwald, November 1, 2020, https://greenwald.substack.com/p/the-ongoing-death-of-free-speech.

20. Greenwald, "The Ongoing Death of Free Speech: Prominent ACLU Lawyer Cheers Suppression of a New Book."

21. Jack Brewster, "The Extremists, Conspiracy Theorists, and Conservative Stars Banned From Social Media Following the Capitol Takeover," *Forbes*, updated January 26, 2021, https://www.forbes.com/sites/jackbrewster/2021/01/12/the-extremists-conspiracy-theorists-and-conservative-stars-banned-from-social-media-following-the-capitol-takeover/?sh=5beae5b968c4.

22. Arthur Bright, "As Tech Giants Recoil From Trump and Parler, Is Free Speech at Risk?," *Christian Science Monitor*, January 11, 2021, https://www.csmonitor.com/USA/Justice/2021/0111/As-tech-giants-recoil-from-Trump-and-Parler-is-free-speech-at-risk.

23. Bruce Haring, "Parler CEO Says Service Dropped by 'Every Vendor' and Could End His Business," Deadline, January 10, 2021, https://deadline.com/2021/01/parler-ceo-says-service-dropped-by-every-vendor-and-could-end-the-company-1234670607/.

24. "Anita Bryant," Wikipedia, last edited April 27, 2021, https://en.wikipedia.org/wiki/Anita_Bryant.

25. "Anita Bryant," Wikipedia.

26. "Anita Bryant," Wikipedia.

27. Julia Manchester, "Majority Says Cancel Culture Poses 'Threat to Freedom,'" *The Hill*, March 1, 2021, https://thehill.com/homenews/campaign/541054-majority-says-cancel-culture-poses-a-threat-to-freedom.

28. Jonathan Cahn, "Jonathan Cahn: Prophetic Message to Joe Biden! (Presidential Inaugural 2020)," YouTube, January 25, 2021, website archived January 26, 2021, https://web.archive.

org/web/20210126172140if_/https://www.youtube.com/
watch?v=hrCtoQUXnmc.

29. Jim Daly with Paul Batura, "Twitter Censors Focus on the Family's
The Daily Citizen," Focus on the Family, January 27, 2021, https://
jimdaly.focusonthefamily.com/twitter-censors-focus-on-the-familys-
the-daily-citizen/.

30. Katie Zezima, "Meet Rachel Levine, One of the Very Few
Transgender Public Officials in America," *Washington Post*,
June 1, 2016, https://www.washingtonpost.com/politics/meet-
rachel-levine-one-of-the-very-few-transgender-public-officials-in-
america/2016/06/01/cf6e2332-2415-11e6-8690-f14ca9de2972_story.
html.

31. Cahn, "Jonathan Cahn."

32. Cahn, "Jonathan Cahn."

33. Dwight D. Eisenhower, "Letter to Robert J. Biggs," Dwight D.
Eisenhower Memorial Commission, February 10, 1959, https://web.
archive.org/web/20081202114605/https://www.eisenhowermemorial.
org/presidential-papers/second-term/documents/1051.cfm.

34. Michael Brown, "How the Left Wants to Eliminate Competing
Ideas," Charisma News, January 19, 2021, https://www.
charismanews.com/opinion/in-the-line-of-fire/84079-how-the-left-
wants-to-eliminate-competing-ideas.

35. "GLAAD Accountability Project," GLAAD, accessed May 6, 2021,
https://www.glaad.org/gap.

36. "Commentator Accountability Project," GLAAD, website archived
March 17, 2012, https://web.archive.org/web/20120317194342/http://
www.glaad.org/cap.

37. Brown, "How the Left Wants to Eliminate Competing Ideas."

38. Jerry McNerney, "Reps. McNerney & Eshoo Urge TV Companies
to Address Spread of Misinformation," news release, February 22,
2021, https://mcnerney.house.gov/media-center/press-releases/reps-
mcnerney-eshoo-urge-tv-companies-to-address-spread-of.

39. Anna G. Eshoo and Jerry McNerney, letter to John T. Stankey,
February 22, 2021, https://docs.house.gov/meetings/IF/
IF16/20210224/111229/HHRG-117-IF16-20210224-SD001.pdf.

40. Molly Ball, "The Secret History of the Shadow Campaign That
Saved the 2020 Election," *Time*, February 4, 2021, https://time.
com/5936036/secret-2020-election-campaign/.

41. "History," National Association of Evangelicals, accessed May 6, 2021, https://www.nae.net/about-nae/history/.

42. Ken Fish, "Cancel Culture Endangers Our American Way of Life, Expert Says," April 15, 2021, in *Strang Report*, podcast, https://www.charismapodcastnetwork.com/show/strangreport/306d3540-d571-4c7c-a1e3-1fe2b4db251d/Cancel-Culture-Endangers-Our-American-Way-of-Life%2C-Expert-Says.

Chapter 2

1. Stephen Strang, "Against Overwhelming Odds: MyPillow Founder Reveals Miraculous Life Transformation Story," *Charisma*, December 18, 2020, https://www.charismamag.com/spirit/supernatural/47337-against-overwhelming-odds-my-pillow-founder-reveals-miraculous-life-transformation-story.

2. Mike Lindell, "The Effects of Cancel Culture With Mike Lindell," March 29, 2021, in *Strang Report*, podcast, https://www.charismapodcastnetwork.com/show/strangreport/2650f41d-8f5c-400f-abf4-007995fb977a/The-Effects-of-Cancel-Culture-with-Mike-Lindell.

3. Jimmy Kimmel Live, "Klan Mom, MyPillow Mike & Courtside Karen Keeping America Great!," YouTube, February 2, 2021, https://www.youtube.com/watch?v=evw0TySlkBw.

4. Lindell, "The Effects of Cancel Culture With Mike Lindell."

5. Lindell, "The Effects of Cancel Culture With Mike Lindell."

6. Taylor Telford, "MyPillow CEO Says Bed Bath & Beyond, Kohl's, Wayfair Are Dropping His Products," *Washington Post*, January 19, 2021, https://www.washingtonpost.com/business/2021/01/19/my-pillow-ceo-lindell/+&cd=10&hl=en&ct=clnk&gl=us.

7. Natalie Colarossi, "Activists Question Walmart, Others Carrying MyPillow Products Over CEO's Response to Capitol Riot," *Newsweek*, January 16, 2021, https://www.newsweek.com/activists-question-walmart-others-carrying-mypillow-products-over-ceos-response-capitol-riot-1562118.

8. Stephen Strang, "Mike Lindell Says the Cancel Culture Is Stealing Our First Amendment Rights, but We Must Not Live in Fear," Charisma News, March 29, 2021, https://www.charismanews.com/us/84894-mike-lindell-says-the-cancel-culture-is-stealing-our-first-amendment-rights-but-we-must-not-live-in-fear.

9. Lindell, "The Effects of Cancel Culture With Mike Lindell."

10. Lindell, "The Effects of Cancel Culture With Mike Lindell."

11. Nick Logan, "How This Credit Card Transaction Company Supports Biblical Values With Nick Logan," January 27, 2021, in *Strang Report*, podcast, https://www.charismapodcastnetwork.com/show/strangreport/6349bab6-0550-470a-90ce-88d6c5ad6265/How-This-Credit-Card-Transaction-Company-Supports-Biblical-Values-with-Nick-Logan.

12. SaveCalifornia.com, "So-called Christian Donation Processing Firm Caves to LGBT Demands and Dumps Christian Ministry, Placing Other Ministry Clients at Same Risk," Campaign for Children and Families, April 4, 2018, https://www.savecalifornia.com/4-4-18-so-called-christian-credit-card-processing-firm-caves-to-lgbt-demands-and-dumps-christian-ministry.html.

13. Logan, "How This Credit Card Transaction Company Supports Biblical Values With Nick Logan"; in communication with the author.

14. Tim Wildmon, "Urgent Message From Tim Wildmon," AFA, archived December 16, 2020, https://web.archive.org/web/20201216151137/https://www.afa.net/urgentupdate.

15. Stephen Strang, "'Babylon Bee' Owner Seth Dillon Shares How Christian Satire Has Now Run Afoul of Cancel Culture," Charisma News, May 10, 2021, https://www.charismanews.com/us/85389-babylon-bee-owner-seth-dillon-shares-how-christian-satire-has-now-run-afoul-of-cancel-culture.

16. Chelsey Cox, "Fact Check: Satirical Claim That the 9th Circuit Court of Appeals Overturned Ginsburg's Death," *USA Today*, updated September 27, 2020, https://www.usatoday.com/story/news/factcheck/2020/09/27/fact-check-only-satire-could-9th-circuit-overturn-ginsburgs-death/3548008001/.

17. Adam Ford (@Adam4d), "There is so much to love about this tweet that I don't know where to start," Twitter, July 24, 2019, 3:49 p.m., https://twitter.com/Adam4d/status/1154156990077263872.

18. Strang, "'Babylon Bee' Owner Seth Dillon Shares How Christian Satire Has Now Run Afoul of Cancel Culture."

19. Svab, "Communist Tactics to Force Self-Censorship Sweeping America."

Chapter 3

1. Joe Biden (@JoeBiden), "We are in the midst of a crisis with the coronavirus. We need to lead the way with science—not Donald Trump's record of hysteria, xenophobia, and fear-mongering. He is the worst possible person to lead our country through a global health emergency," Twitter, February 1, 2020, 5:01 p.m., https://twitter.com/JoeBiden/status/1223727977361338370.

2. Katie Rogers, "'Border Security Is Also Health Security,' Trump Says at Rally as Coronavirus Fears Grow," *New York Times*, February 29, 2020, https://www.nytimes.com/2020/02/29/us/politics/trump-rally-coronavirus.html.

3. Fox News, "EXCLUSIVE: Trump goes one-on-one with Hannity to discuss coronavirus response," YouTube, March 26, 2020, https://www.youtube.com/watch?v=A6Jd-e1vUoA&t=4s.

4. "American Eyewitness: COVID-19 is Worse Than Chinese Government Will Admit," Strang Report, February 20, 2020, https://strangreport.libsyn.com/alexandra-rodriguez.

5. Stephen Strang, "Prayers and Prophecies to Push Back Against the Coronavirus," Strang Report, March 9, 2020, https://strangreport.libsyn.com/prayers-and-prophecies-to-push-back-against-the-coronavirus.

6. Charisma News Staff, "COVID-Busting Warrior Physician Stella Immanuel: 'America, You Don't Need to Be Afraid,'" Charisma News, July 29, 2020, https://www.charismanews.com/us/82067-covid-busting-warrior-physician-stella-immanuel-america-you-don-t-need-to-be-afraid.

7. Charisma News Staff, "Frontline Physician Stella Immanuel: 'I Maintain That There Is a Cure for COVID,'" Charisma News, August 6, 2020, https://www.charismamag.com/life/health/46186-frontline-physician-stella-immanuel-i-maintain-that-there-is-a-cure-for-covid.

8. Allum Bokhari, "Facebook, Google/YouTube, Twitter Censor Viral Video of Doctors' Capitol Hill Coronavirus Press Conference," Breitbart, July 27, 2020, https://www.breitbart.com/tech/2020/07/27/facebook-censors-viral-video-of-doctors-capitol-hill-coronavirus-press-conference/#.

9. Jim Hoft, "Doctor Simone Gold Fired From Hospital After Attending 'White Coat Summit' -- Hires Atty Lin

Wood," YouTube, July 30, 2020, https://www.youtube.com/watch?v=tynTVhyGxiI.

10. Ivory Hecker, "Doctor's Controversial Claim of COVID-19 Cure Goes Viral, Gets Censored," Fox 26 Houston, July 28, 2020, https://www.fox26houston.com/news/doctors-controversial-claim-of-covid-19-cure-goes-viral-gets-censored.

11. Charisma News Staff, "COVID-Busting Warrior Physician Stella Immanuel."

12. "America's Frontline Doctors SCOTUS Press Conference Transcript," Rev, July 27, 2020, https://www.rev.com/blog/transcripts/americas-frontline-doctors-scotus-press-conference-transcript.

13. Hoft, "Doctor Simone Gold Fired from Hospital After Attending 'White Coat Summit.'

14. CNBC, "Pres. Donald Trump: I'm taking hydroxychloroquine to prevent coronavirus infection," YouTube, May 18, 2020, https://www.youtube.com/watch?v=7nkwE3didNo.

15. Emily Bary, "Twitter suspends Donald Trump Jr.'s account for 12 hours over hydroxychloroquine tweet," MarketWatch, July 28, 2020, https://www.marketwatch.com/story/twitter-suspends-donald-trump-jrs-account-for-12-hours-over-hydroxychloroquine-tweet-2020-07-28.

16. Nick Robins-Early, Hayley Miller, and Jesselyn Cook, "How Quack Doctors and Powerful GOP Operatives Spread Misinformation to Millions," HuffPost, updated July 29, 2020, https://www.huffpost.com/entry/how-quack-doctors-and-powerful-gop-operatives-spread-misinformation-to-millions_n_5f208048c5b66859f1f33148.

17. Ryan W. Miller and Joel Shannon, "'America's Frontline Doctors' may be real doctors, but experts say they don't know what they're talking about," *USA Today*, updated July 31, 2020, https://www.usatoday.com/story/news/nation/2020/07/30/americas-frontline-doctors-tout-hydroxychloroquine-covid-who-they/5535096002/.

18. Charisma News Staff, "Frontline Physician Stella Immanuel."

19. Stella Immanuel, "Big Tech is censoring Experts and suppressing the CURE. I will not be silenced. #HCQWorks pic.twitter.com/fenaM9FDHV—Stella Immanuel MD (@stella_immanuel) July 28, 2020," Twitter, July 28, 2020. Twitter removed the tweet and suspended the account.

20. Dale Hurd, "Why the Smear Campaign Against Hydroxychloroquine?," CBN News, August 10, 2020, https://www1.

cbn.com/cbnnews/us/2020/august/why-the-smear-campaign-against-hydroxychloroquine.

21. As of May 10, 2020, WHO reported 165,419 cases in Nigeria, or only 0.08% of the population, and 32,334,764 cases in the US, or 9.8% of the population. "WHO Coronavirus Dashboard: Situation by Region, Country, Territory & Area," WHO, accessed May 10, 2020, https://covid19.who.int/table.

22. Charisma News Staff, "Frontline Physician Stella Immanuel."

23. Charisma News Staff, "Frontline Physician Stella Immanuel."

24. "Homepage," Mercola, accessed May 10, 2021, https://www.mercola.com/.

25. Joseph Mercola, "The Truth About COVID-19," Mercola, May 1, 2021, https://articles.mercola.com/sites/articles/archive/2021/05/01/dave-asprey-interview-the-truth-about-covid-19.aspx. Mercola's article was still online at the time of this writing, but Google seemed to be making it difficult to find. A search for specific phrases from the article brought up no links to Mercola's website, only to third parties that reposted the op-ed.

26. Hoft, "Doctor Simone Gold Fired From Hospital After Attending 'White Coat Summit.'"

27. Hurd, "Why the Smear Campaign Against Hydroxychloroquine?"

Chapter 4

1. National Association of Realtors, "2021 Code of Ethics & Standards of Practice," accessed May 11, 2021, https://www.nar.realtor/about-nar/governing-documents/code-of-ethics/2021-code-of-ethics-standards-of-practice.

2. Mike Bickle, "The Comparison of Today's Culture Persecution to Ancient Prophecy With Mike Bickle," April 16, 2021, in *Strang Report*, podcast, https://strangreport.libsyn.com/-sr-mike-bickle.

3. I am proud of the fact that I was able to do a story on healing evangelist Kathryn Kuhlman, which they made a cover story for the Sunday magazine.

4. Fish, "Cancel Culture Endangers Our American Way of Life, Expert Says."

5. Daniel Bell, *The Coming of Post-Industrial Society* (New York: Basic Books, 1999), 480, https://archive.org/details/comingofpostindu00bell_0/page/n7/mode/2up.

6. Francis Schaeffer, *How Should We Then Live?*, episode 10, "Final Choices," 1977, https://www.amazon.com/How-Should-We-Then-Live/dp/B075X9KTHG.

7. Ed Stetzer, "Unliked Likes: Cancelling Pastor Chris Hodges and Church of the Highlands," Christianity Today, June 11, 2020, https://www.christianitytoday.com/edstetzer/2020/june/chris-hodges-trump-kirk-cancel-culture.html.

8. Evangelical Alliance, "Starmer's Treatment of Jesus House Is a 'Concerted Attack' on Freedom of Religion," Evangelical Alliance, April 9, 2021, https://www.eauk.org/news-and-views/starmers-treatment-of-jesus-house-is-a-concerted-attack-on-freedom-of-religion.

9. Gavin Calver, "Faith Leader's Solution to Cancel Culture: Uncompromising Faith, Unconditional Love with Gavin Calver," April 23, 2021, in *Strang Report*, podcast, https://www.charismapodcastnetwork.com/show/strangreport/6c724919-7f94-4479-8caf-eab906def9ea/Faith-Leader's-Solution-to-Cancel-Culture%3A-Uncompromising-Faith%2C-Unconditional-Love-with-Gavin-Calver.

10. Evangelical Alliance, "Starmer's Treatment of Jesus House Is a 'Concerted Attack' on Freedom of Religion."

11. "Pastor Told Not to Offend Gay Pride as Mob Threaten to Burn Down His Church," Christian Concern, September 8, 2020, https://christianconcern.com/news/pastor-told-not-to-offend-gay-pride-as-mob-threaten-to-burn-down-his-church/.

12. Schaeffer, *How Should We Then Live?*

13. John Burton, "Big Tech Censorship Means a New Social Media Game Plan for Christians," Charisma News, February 8, 2021, https://www.charismanews.com/culture/84312-big-tech-censorship-means-a-new-social-media-game-plan-for-christians.

14. Jacob Bogage, "Companies celebrate the Supreme Court's same-sex marriage ruling," *Washington Post*, June 26, 2015, https://www.washingtonpost.com/news/wonk/wp/2015/06/26/companies-celebrate-the-supreme-courts-same-sex-marriage-ruling/.

15. David Lane, "When Christians Disengaged Culture, the Antichrist Spirit Stepped In," Charisma News, April 15, 2019, https://www.charismanews.com/opinion/renewing-america/75949-when-christians-disengaged-culture-the-antichrist-spirit-stepped-in.

16. Burton, "Big Tech Censorship Means a New Social Media Game Plan for Christians."

17. Andrew Torba, "The Problem With the American Populist Movement Is That It Was Centralized," Restoring Liberty, February 19, 2021, https://joemiller.us/2021/02/the-problem-with-the-american-populist-movement-is-that-it-was-centralized/?utm_source=rss&utm_medium=rss&utm_campaign=the-problem-with-the-american-populist-movement-is-that-it-was-centralized.

18. Trevor Loudon, "A New Zealander's 9 'Starter Steps' to Save America From Socialism," *Epoch Times*, updated March 11, 2021, https://www.theepochtimes.com/a-new-zealanders-9-starter-steps-to-save-america-from-socialism_3718917.html.

19. Fish, "Cancel Culture Endangers Our American Way of Life."

Chapter 5

1. Eric Metaxas, "Why Eric Metaxas Says Now More Than Ever, Americans Must Avoid Evils of Communism," May 4, 2021, in *Strang Report*, podcast, https://www.charismapodcastnetwork.com/show/strangreport/52aa1f0e-8d4f-40be-ad42-5a05efffbb49/Why-Eric-Metaxas-Says-Now-More-Than-Ever%2C-Americans-Must-Avoid-Evils-of-Communism.

2. Metaxas, "Why Eric Metaxas Says Now More Than Ever, Americans Must Avoid Evils of Communism."

3. Loudon, "A New Zealander's 9 'Starter Steps' to Save America From Socialism."

4. Trevor Loudon, "Trevor Loudon Addresses the Question: Are We Going Through a Marxist, Lenin-Style Takeover?," April 26, 2021, in *Strang Report*, podcast, https://www.charismapodcastnetwork.com/show/strangreport/ce261fc4-bd8e-4532-bb93-7c19ccaa587a/Trevor-Loudon-Addresses-the-Question%3A-Are-We-Going-Through-a-Marxist%2C-Lenin-Style-Takeover%3F.

5. Charles Creitz, "Trump Jr. warns election is 'about freedom versus tyranny, capitalism versus socialism and Communism,'" Fox News, October 28, 2019, https://www.foxnews.com/politics/donald-trump-jr-2020-election-freedom-tyranny-capitalism-socialism.

6. Loudon, "Trevor Loudon Addresses the Question."

7. Wead, "Doug Wead Says Christianity Is 'First Thing They Want to Silence.'"

8. Loudon, "Trevor Loudon Addresses the Question."

9. Rob McCoy, "California Pastor Rob McCoy Advances Freedom Fight, Sees Explosive Church Growth," April 27, 2021, in *Strang Report*, podcast, https://www.charismapodcastnetwork.com/show/strangreport/76ea4c4b-382d-4bf0-a291-e1711b765d7a/California-Pastor-Rob-McCoy-Advances-Freedom-Fight%2C-Sees-Explosive-Church-Growth.

10. Kilpatrick, "The Cancel Culture With Joel Kilpatrick."

11. Loudon, "Trevor Loudon Addresses the Question."

12. Eric Metaxas, interview with author, April 20, 2021.

13. Fish, "Cancel Culture Endangers Our American Way of Life."

Chapter 6

1. Abraham Lincoln, "Second Inaugural Address," March 4, 1865, National Park Service, https://www.nps.gov/linc/learn/historyculture/lincoln-second-inaugural.htm.

2. Rick Joyner, "Be Prepared for a Second Coming American Revolution and Civil War With Rick Joyner," April 20, 2021, in *Strang Report*, podcast, https://www.charismapodcastnetwork.com/show/strangreport/64787387-8ba5-4d58-a2ca-a9dd5625806b/Be-Prepared-for-a-Second-Coming-American-Revolution-and-Civil-War-with-Rick-Joyner.

3. Bob Jones, "2020-03D The Perfect Storm by Bob Jones With Bonnie Jones Intro and Recap," YouTube, March 23, 2020, https://www.youtube.com/watch?v=IQIcuOFO36Q.

4. Joyner, "Be Prepared for a Second Coming American Revolution and Civil War With Rick Joyner."

5. "Sid Roth 998 Joyner," Sid Roth, accessed May 13, 2021, https://sidroth.org/wp-content/uploads/2019/04/IS998Transcript_Joyner.pdf.

6. SermonIndex.net, "David Wilkerson Prophecy - New York 1000 Fires," YouTube, April 18, 2012, https://www.youtube.com/watch?v=iodpg6sDtcs.

7. Yustos Anthony, "Mike Bickle's open vision about America," YouTube, January 2, 2009, https://www.youtube.com/watch?v=eLZpsepaVcM.

8. Larry Reid Live, "Pastor Dana Coverstone shares his prophetic dreams from 6.22.20 about COVID-19, The Election and . .," YouTube, July 9, 2020, https://www.youtube.com/watch?v=SAZGxTiX6bY.

9. John Paul Jackson, "The Perfect Storm (eBooklet)," SlideShare, accessed May 13, 2021, https://www.slideshare.net/k24s3/thecomingperfectstormjohnpauljackson; Streams Ministries, "The Perfect Storm," YouTube, July 27, 2016, https://www.youtube.com/watch?v=kzPJjOxZorg.

10. They also host a prayer meeting for the nation and a church service on Friday evenings in Palm Coast, Florida, not far from where I live.

11. JackRigney, "Donna Rigney Ministries, September 8, 2019 Revelations from the Mountain of Intimacy," YouTube, September 17, 2019, https://www.youtube.com/watch?v=Ioyvv3jXZc4.

12. ElijahStreams, "DONNA RIGNEY: A GREAT UNVEILING IS COMING!," YouTube, April 2, 2021, https://www.youtube.com/watch?v=e_AneBruIGk.

13. Joyner, "Be Prepared for a Second Coming American Revolution and Civil War With Rick Joyner."

14. Loudon, "A New Zealander's 9 'Starter Steps' to Save America From Socialism."

15. KTLA 5, "'You are right to feel wronged': Newsom responds to weekend violence," YouTube, June 1, 2020, https://www.youtube.com/watch?v=va7rl5seIXQ.

16. Adam Edelman, "Biden slams Capitol rioters as 'domestic terrorists': 'Don't dare call them protesters,'" NBC News, updated January 7, 2021, https://www.nbcnews.com/politics/white-house/biden-slams-capitol-rioters-domestic-terrorists-don-t-dare-call-n1253335.

17. Loudon, "A New Zealander's 9 'Starter Steps' to Save America From Socialism."

18. Joyner, "Be Prepared for a Second Coming American Revolution and Civil War With Rick Joyner."

19. Jackson, "The Perfect Storm."

20. Joyner, "Be Prepared for a Second Coming American Revolution and Civil War With Rick Joyner."

21. Jones, "2020-03D The Perfect Storm by Bob Jones with Bonnie Jones Intro and Recap."

22. Jackson, "The Perfect Storm."

Chapter 7

1. Soumya Karlamangla, "Mass Shooting in Thousand Oaks eclipsed by huge wildfires, families and friends of victims say," *Los Angeles Times*, November 18, 2018, https://www.latimes.com/local/california/la-me-ln-thousand-oaks-shooting-follow-20181118-story.html.

2. Chris Roberts, "How Cannabis (Accidentally) Helped Churches Reopen During the COVID Pandemic," *Forbes*, August 26, 2020, https://www.forbes.com/sites/chrisroberts/2020/08/26/how-cannabis-accidentally-helped-reopen-churches-during-the-covid-pandemic/?sh=617697c246c4.

3. "Governor Gavin Newsom Issues Stay at Home Order," Office of Governor Gavin Newsom, March 19, 2020, https://www.gov.ca.gov/2020/03/19/governor-gavin-newsom-issues-stay-at-home-order/.

4. Andrew Court, "'Satan's Trying to Keep Us Apart!' Dozens of Defiant Christian Pastors Will Hold Palm Sunday Services Despite Orders to Self-Isolate Amid the Coronavirus Crisis," Daily Mail, updated April 5, 2020, https://www.dailymail.co.uk/news/article-8187755/The-Americans-defying-Palm-Sunday-quarantines-Satans-trying-apart.html.

5. "County of Ventura, California: Adopted Budget, Fiscal Year 2019-20," County of Ventura, accessed May 14, 2021, https://vcportal.ventura.org/auditor/docs/adopted-budgets/fy2019-2020/1.%20%20Full%20Report/1.%20%20Adopted%20Budget%202020%20excluding%20Appendix%20C.pdf.

6. Kilpatrick, "The Cancel Culture With Joel Kilpatrick."

7. Kathleen Wilson, "Leader of COVID Response in Ventura County Gets Pay Increase," *VC Star*, updated November 14, 2020, https://www.vcstar.com/story/news/2020/11/13/dr-levin-covid-ventura-county-public-health-officer-pay-increase/6217673002/.

8. KTLA 5, "Coronavirus: Ventura County officials expand testing to symptomatic, some asymptomatic people," YouTube, May 4, 2020, https://www.youtube.com/watch?v=0Kf_gWrBio4.

9. County of Ventura, "COVID-19 Press Conference—May 6, 2020," Facebook, May 6, 2020, https://www.facebook.com/watch/live/?v=576960452941376&ref=watch_permalink.

10. Kilpatrick, "The Cancel Culture With Joel Kilpatrick."

11. Joel Kilpatrick, "County Health Officer Wants to Monitor Citizens for COVID-19 Exposure," May 8, 2020, in *Strang Report*, podcast, https://strangreport.libsyn.com/local-county-health-officer-wants-to-montor-citizens-for-covid-19-exposure.

12. "Residents Concerned, Shocked by Ventura County's Plans to Isolate, Quarantine," *Conejo Guardian,* June 28, 2020, https://www.conejoguardian.org/2020/06/28/residents-concerned-shocked-by-ventura-county-plans-to-isolate-quarantine/.

13. Kilpatrick, "The Cancel Culture With Joel Kilpatrick."

14. Kathleen Wilson, "County Sues Pastor, Newbury Park Church for Court Order to Stop Large Indoor Services," Vc Star, updated August 5, 2020, https://www.vcstar.com/story/news/2020/08/04/ventura-county-covid-enforcement-actions-approved-supervisors/3296096001/; Becca Whitnall, "Judge Rejects Request to Lock Down Church," Moorpark Acorn, August 11, 2020, https://www.mpacorn.com/articles/judge-rejects-request-to-lock-down-church/.

15. "California Pastor Vows to Hold Indoor Worship Despite Order," Associated Press, August 8, 2020, https://apnews.com/article/virus-outbreak-california-public-health-courts-6945cfac131048f2106ca9ad f7079e5e.

16. McCoy, "California Pastor Rob McCoy Advances Freedom Fight."

17. Dylan Matthews, "Whitewater, Explained for people who don't remember the Clinton presidency," Vox, April 13, 2015, https://www.vox.com/2015/4/13/8397309/hillary-clinton-whitewater.

18. "Congressional Record, Proceedings and Debates of the 83rd Congress, Second Session, Volume 100-Part 7," United States Congress, July 2, 1954, https://www.congress.gov/83/crecb/1954/07/02/GPO-CRECB-1954-pt7-9.pdf, 9604.

19. Editorial Board, "Trump Is Wrong. Pulpit Freedom Already Exists," *Washington Post*, August 5, 2016, https://www.washingtonpost.com/opinions/trump-is-wrong-pulpit-freedom-already-exists/2016/08/05/77706c10-5815-11e6-9aee-8075993d73a2_story.html.

20. "The Legal Implications of the Johnson Amendment," Alliance Defending Freedom, October 17, 2017, https://adflegal.org/blog/legal-implications-johnson-amendment.

21. Blue Letter Bible, s.v. *"ekklēsia,"* accessed May 14, 2021, https://www.blueletterbible.org/lang/lexicon/lexicon.cfm?t=kjv&strongs=g1577.

22. Aristotle, *Politics*, 1.1, trans. Benjamin Jowett, accessed May 14, 2021, http://classics.mit.edu/Aristotle/politics.1.one.html.

23. McCoy, "California Pastor Rob McCoy Advances Freedom Fight."

24. "SCOTUS Ends CA's Total Worship Ban," Liberty Counsel, February 6, 2021, https://lc.org/newsroom/details/020621-scotus-ends-cas-total-worship-ban-1.

25. Shannon Grove, "California Sen. Shannon Grove: 'The Government Is Coming After Our Pastors,'" October 16, 2020, in *Strang Report*, podcast, https://www.charismapodcastnetwork.com/show/strangreport/7f1a4cca-b934-4a8b-9ca1-956d06865269/California-Sen.-Shannon-Grove%3A-'The-Government-Is-Coming-After-Our-Pastors'.

26. *Rocky III*, directed by Sylvester Stallone (Los Angeles, CA: MGM/UA Entertainment Co., 1982).

27. Bill Johnson, interview with author, April 20, 2021; Bill Johnson, "What Do You Do When Government Authority Is in the Wrong? Interview With Bill Johnson," May 19, 2021, in *Strang Report*, podcast, https://www.charismapodcastnetwork.com/show/strangreport/d399d038-928f-49de-848d-adca6247d2be/What-Do-You-Do-When-Government-Authority-Is-In-the-Wrong%3F-Interview-with-Bill-Johnson.

28. George Washington, "Farewell Address," September 19, 1796, https://www.ourdocuments.gov/doc.php?flash=false&doc=15.

29. Joyner, "Be Prepared for a Second Coming American Revolution and Civil War With Rick Joyner."

30. Loudon, "Trevor Loudon Addresses the Question."

31. Loudon, "A New Zealander's 9 'Starter Steps' to Save America From Socialism."

32. "Nullification: What factors prompt states to override federal laws?," Texas A&M, March 19, 2018, https://research.tamu.edu/2018/03/19/nullification-what-factors-prompt-states-to-override-federal-laws/; "State of the Nullification Movement: 2019-10 Tenth Amendment Center Annual Report," Tenth Amendment Center, accessed May 15, 2021, https://s3.amazonaws.com/TAChandbooks/2019-20-state-of-the-nullification-movement-report.pdf.

33. Loudon, "Trevor Loudon Addresses the Question."

34. Debra Tash, "Superior Court Judge Rules Godspeak Calvary in Contempt; $3,000 fine; Ventura County drops sanctions against congregation members," Citizens Journal, August 21, 2020, https://

www.citizensjournal.us/superior-court-judge-rules-godspeak-calvary-in-contempt-3000-fine-ventura-county-drops-sanctions-against-congregation-members/.

35. *County of Ventura and Robert Levin, M.D., in his capacity as Health Officer for Ventura County, vs. Godspeak Calvary Chapel, Rob Mccoy and DOES 1-1000, inclusive* (August 21, 2020) (statement of Hon. Vincent J. O'Neill, Jr., Ventura County Superior Court). In his decision, Judge Vincent J. O'Neill said, "All right. Well, it's, indeed, an unpleasant—the issues are narrow today, as I mentioned at the start. I fully understand that there's a reason that freedom of religion is protected by the very First Amendment. But I have a duty to uphold the Court's order that was duly issued. And so I find both Pastor McCoy and the church, as a body, in contempt of the Superior Court's order. There is jurisdiction for the order. There is knowledge of it and the ability to comply. And, clearly, willful disobedience; although, well-motivated. And on the ability to comply, I think it is significant that there are other options here. It is not the government telling people not to worship or even congregate. And so there's clearly an element here of establishing a test case, and that's not a defense to violating a Court order."

36. "The Only Thing Necessary for the Triumph of Evil Is That Good Men Do Nothing," Quote Investigator, December 4, 2010, https://quoteinvestigator.com/2010/12/04/good-men-do/.

37. McCoy, "California Pastor Rob McCoy Advances Freedom Fight."

Chapter 8

1. Bickle, "The Comparison of Today's Culture Persecution to Ancient Prophecy With Mike Bickle."

2. David Russell Schilling, "Knowledge Doubling Every 12 Months, Soon to Be Every 12 Hours," Industry Tap, April 19, 2013, https://www.industrytap.com/knowledge-doubling-every-12-months-soon-to-be-every-12-hours/3950.

3. Bickle, "The Comparison of Today's Culture Persecution to Ancient Prophecy With Mike Bickle."

4. Wead, "Doug Wead Says Christianity Is 'First Thing They Want to Silence.'"

5. Fish, "Cancel Culture Endangers Our American Way of Life."

6. Charles Crismier, "How Globalism Is Preparing the Way for the Antichrist With Chuck Crismier," March 24, 2021, in *Strang Report*, podcast, https://www.charismapodcastnetwork.com/show/strangreport/7260dc91-6853-4c0c-b0ac-ec9c73736a31/How-Globalism-Is-Preparing-the-Way-for-the-Antichrist-with-Chuck-Crismier.

7. CBN News, "Pastor Brunson Predicts Intensified Persecution of U.S. Christians," YouTube, December 11, 2020, https://www.youtube.com/watch?v=teBUjhLlqhs&t=17s; Used with permission; Andrew Brunson, in communication with the author, May 11, 2021.

8. Kilpatrick, "The Cancel Culture With Joel Kilpatrick."

9. Michele Bachmann, "How the Pilgrims Started With a Prayer Meeting With Michele Bachmann," November 12, 2020, in *Strang Report*, podcast, https://www.charismapodcastnetwork.com/show/strangreport/14c1e0d2-39c6-43cc-84eb-2bbf517cd1f1/How-the-Pilgrims-Started-with-a-Prayer-Meeting-with-Michele-Bachmann.

10. "The Mayflower Compact," Pilgrim Hall Museum, November 21, 1620, https://www.pilgrimhall.org/ap_mayflower_compact.htm.

11. Jon Hamill, "New Mayflower Compact Signing Highlights Prophetic Influence of Pilgrim Fathers," November 23, 2020, in *Strang Report*, podcast, https://www.charismapodcastnetwork.com/show/strangreport/773c932c-ae3d-4ff0-8a36-0416261826e5/New-Mayflower-Compact-Signing-Highlights-Prophetic-Influence-of-Pilgrim-Fathers.

12. Bickle, "The Comparison of Today's Culture Persecution to Ancient Prophecy With Mike Bickle."

Chapter 9

1. Greg Fairrington, "Greg Fairrington Takes a Stand to Keep Churches Open During the Pandemic," May 24, 2021, in *Strang Report*, podcast, https://strangreport.libsyn.com/greg-farrington.

2. Fairrington, "Greg Fairrington Takes a Stand to Keep Churches Open During the Pandemic."

3. Marlee Ginter, "Megachurch Hosts Large Crowd For New Year's Eve Wedding," CBS Sacramento, January 1, 2021, https://sacramento.cbslocal.com/2021/01/01/

rocklin-megachurch-hosts-large-crowd-for-new-years-eve-wedding/;
Michael McGough, "California Church With History of Flouting
COVID Rules Set to Host New Year's Wedding," *Sacramento Bee*,
December 31, 2020, https://www.sacbee.com/news/coronavirus/
article248194890.html.

4. Dale Kasler, "'Biblical mandate.' California Churches Ready
to Defy Newsom After Supreme Court Ruling," *Sacramento
Bee*, updated December 1, 2020, https://www.sacbee.com/news/
california/article247507750.html.

5. Hemant Mehta, "Christian Death Cult Pastor: 'Never Again Will
the Church Shut Its Doors,'" *Friendly Atheist*, March 9, 2021,
https://friendlyatheist.patheos.com/2021/03/09/christian-death-
cult-pastor-never-again-will-the-church-shut-its-doors/.

6. Fairrington, "Greg Fairrington Takes a Stand to Keep Churches
Open During the Pandemic."

7. Fairrington, "Greg Fairrington Takes a Stand to Keep Churches
Open During the Pandemic."

8. Joel Kilpatrick, "Here is what I see coming for the Christian
community nationwide," Facebook, May 27, 2020,
7:21 p.m., https://www.facebook.com/joel.kilpatrick.9/
posts/10158568877539343.

9. Kilpatrick, "The Cancel Culture With Joel Kilpatrick."

10. Fairrington, "Greg Fairrington Takes a Stand to Keep Churches
Open During the Pandemic."

11. David Lane, "America Is Besieged by the Opposing but
Cohabiting Forces of Human Secularism, Political Correctness and
Multiculturalism," Constant Contact, accessed May 18, 2021, https://
myemail.constantcontact.com/-everything-anti-Christ.html?soid=110
6253726374&aid=Wq2lZKVgrKk.

12. Mario Murillo, "What Should the Church's Response Be to the
Political Pillar With Mario Murillo," May 11, 2021, in *Strang
Report*, podcast, https://www.charismapodcastnetwork.com/show/
strangreport/91e96e4d-bb98-4146-a1d6-d8f85f7013de/What-Should-
the-Church's-Response-Be-to-the-Political-Pillar-with-Mario-Murillo.

13. Justin Mason, "WWII pilot remembers Flying Fortress," *Daily
Gazette*, October 4, 2008, https://dailygazette.com/2008/10/04/1004_
wwiipilot/.

14. Murillo, "What Should the Church's Response Be to the Political
Pillar With Mario Murillo."

15. Johnson, "What Do You Do When Government Authority Is in the Wrong? Interview With Bill Johnson."

16. Francis Schaeffer, *How Should We Then Live?*, episode 9, "The Age of Personal Peace and Affluence," 1977, https://www.amazon.com/How-Should-We-Then-Live/dp/B075X9KTHG.

17. Schaeffer, *How Should We Then Live?*, episode 10, "Final Choices," 1977, https://www.amazon.com/How-Should-We-Then-Live/dp/B075X9KTHG.

18. Joyner, "Be Prepared for a Second Coming American Revolution and Civil War With Rick Joyner."

19. McCoy, "California Pastor Rob McCoy Advances Freedom Fight."

20. Rheana Murray, "More People Are Going Hungry Than Ever Before. Inside the Efforts to Help," Today, December 15, 2020, https://www.today.com/food/50-million-people-may-experience-hunger-year-these-organizations-are-t203672.

21. Dave Donaldson, Wendell Vinson, and Darren Delaune, "Faith-Based Initiative CityServe Helps Link Families and Farmers in a Season of Need," March 12, 2021, in *Strang Report*, podcast, https://www.charismapodcastnetwork.com/show/strangreport/6433d736-f64d-4af0-8384-73d57d7dcea1/Faith-Based-Initiative-CityServe-Helps-Link-Families-and-Farmers-in-a-Season-of-Need.

22. CityServe is equipping ministries to be part of its HUB and POD distribution model. HUBs are churches or organizations with the capacity to be distribution centers for local churches, known as PODs (points of distribution). CityServe's initiative at Grand Canyon University will equip, resource, and mobilize thousands of students to help local churches reach their neighbors.

23. "Worship," City Church, accessed May 18, 2021, https://citychurchfl.org/worship/.

24. Hal Donaldson, in communication with the author, April 27, 2021; Hal Donaldson, "There Is Power in a Simple Act of Kindness With Hal Donaldson," June 17, 2020, in *Strang Report*, podcast, https://www.charismapodcastnetwork.com/show/strangreport/b893f138-8d64-4eed-a816-48fb75a9a627/There-is-Power-In-A-Simple-Act-of-Kindness-with-Hal-Donaldson.

25. "Unstoppable: 2020 Couldn't Hold Back Your Kindness," Convoy of Hope, accessed May 18, 2021, https://www.convoyofhope.org/blog/features/field-story/2020-year-in-review/.

26. Fairrington, "Greg Fairrington Takes a Stand to Keep Churches Open During the Pandemic."

27. Wead, "Doug Wead Says Christianity Is 'First Thing They Want to Silence.'"

Chapter 10

1. Murillo, "What Should the Church's Response Be to the Political Pillar With Mario Murillo."

2. Chris Reed, "How the Church Has Lost the Fear of the Lord With Chris Reed (Part 1)," May 5, 2021, in *Strang Report*, podcast, https://www.charismapodcastnetwork.com/show/ strangreport/eec2cf92-d168-4f80-9fb1-291cf394e5f0/How-The- Church-Has-Lost-the-Fear-of-the-Lord-with-Chris-Reed-(Part-1).

3. R. T. Kendall, "We've Never Been This Way Before With RT Kendall," October 15, 2020, in *Strang Report*, podcast, https:// www.charismapodcastnetwork.com/show/strangreport/505b298d- fcd2-49da-89b6-f9b5497b089d/We've-Never-Been-This-Way- Before-with-RT-Kendall.

4. Joseph Hudak, "Jesus Christ, Superspreader?," *Rolling Stone*, October 12, 2020, https://www.rollingstone.com/culture/culture- news/sean-feucht-preacher-covid-1074213/.

5. Meagan Clark, "COVID-19 Is Fueling a New Jesus Movement," Religion Unplugged, October 24, 2020, https://religionunplugged. com/news/2020/10/24/how-covid-19-is-fueling-a-new-jesus- movement.

6. Danielle Wallace, "Seattle Christians Confronted by Knife- Wielding Protesters Yelling Obscenities at Black Pastors: Leader," Fox News, August 11, 2020, https://www.foxnews.com/us/seattle- chop-christians-worship-violent-protesters-knives.

7. Mario Murillo, "Now is the Time for the Church to Find Its Moral Spine With Mario Murillo," November 30, 2020, in *Strang Report*, podcast, https://www.charismapodcastnetwork.com/show/ strangreport/9bd1372e-bb4e-4a52-9092-846a78edade7/Now-is- the-Time-for-the-Church-to-Find-Its-Moral-Spine-with-Mario- Murillo.

8. Jane Hamon, "Apostle Jane Hamon Says God Intends Current Crisis to Yield Pandemic of Revival," November 24, 2020, in *Strang Report*, podcast, https://www.charismapodcastnetwork.

com/show/strangreport/751557f6-15af-4cd0-bbec-9ec15cefd409/
Apostle-Jane-Hamon-Says-God-Intends-Current-Crisis-to-Yield-
Pandemic-of-Revival.

9. "Official Statement Regarding the Lawsuit Against Gov. Newsom," Harvest Rock Church, accessed May 19, 2021, https://harvestrock. church/official-statement-regarding-the-lawsuit-against-gov-newsom/.

10. Jeff Struss, "Florida Pastors Gathering Reveals How Rumblings of Revival Are Shaking America," Charisma News, March 15, 2021, https://www.charismanews.com/culture/84735-florida-pastors-gathering-reveals-how-rumblings-of-revival-are-shaking-america.

11. Struss, "Florida Pastors Gathering Reveals How Rumblings of Revival Are Shaking America."

12. Reed, "How the Church Has Lost the Fear of the Lord With Chris Reed."

13. Max Weber, *The Protestant Ethic and the Spirit of Capitalism*, trans. Talcott Parsons (New York: Charles Scribner's Sons, 1958), https:// archive.org/details/protestantethics00weberich.

14. Fish, "Cancel Culture Endangers Our American Way of Life."

15. Wead, "Doug Wead Says Christianity Is 'First Thing They Want to Silence.'"

16. Schaeffer, *How Should We Then Live?*, episode 10.

17. Blue Letter Bible, s.v. "*maranatha*," accessed May 19, 2021, https://www.blueletterbible.org/lang/lexicon/lexicon. cfm?Strongs=G3134&t=KJV.

18. Wead, "Doug Wead Says Christianity Is 'First Thing They Want to Silence.'"

Conclusion

1. Tony Perkins, "Revealing a Conspiracy and Then Facing the 'Cancel Culture,'" Facebook, February 1, 2021, https://www. facebook.com/watch/?v=216213290213999.

2. "Philadelphia Statement," Philadelphia Statement, accessed May 19, 2021, https://thephillystatement.org/read/.

3. "In a Time of Universal Deceit—Telling the Truth Is a Revolutionary Act," Quote Investigator, February 24, 2013, https://quoteinvestigator.com/2013/02/24/truth-revolutionary/.

4. Murillo, "What Should the Church's Response Be to the Political Pillar With Mario Murillo."
5. "The Only Thing Necessary for the Triumph of Evil Is That Good Men Do Nothing," Quote Investigator.

Epilogue

1. "About," Jerusalem Prayer Team, accessed June 4, 2021, https://www.jerusalemprayerteam.org/about/.
2. Andrew Brunson, "Andrew Brunson Shares How He Spiritually Broke Within a Turkish Prison," May 31, 2021, in *Strang Report*, podcast, https://www.charismapodcastnetwork.com/show/strangreport/676cc923-9a22-43b0-937d-0f6d1771df3f/Andrew-Brunson-Shares-How-He-Spiritually-Broke-Within-a-Turkish-Prison.
3. John Paul Jackson, "The Perfect Storm (eBooklet)," SlideShare, accessed May 13, 2021, https://www.slideshare.net/k24s3/thecomingperfectstormjohnpauljackson.

Appendix A

1. Jonathan Cahn, "Jonathan Cahn's Prophetic Message to Joe Biden (Presidential Inauguration 2021)," YouTube, January 25, 2021, https://www.youtube.com/watch?v=hrCtoQUXnmc.

Appendix B

1. "Philadelphia Statement," Philadelphia Statement, accessed May 19, 2021, https://thephillystatement.org/read/. Used with permission. See also Frederick Douglass, "Plea for Free Speech in Boston," Patriot Post, December 10, 1860, https://patriotpost.us/documents/139.

INDEX

My FREE GIFT to You

I'm so glad you read my book. God has great plans and purposes for you, and your calling is active, purposeful, and energetic as you take back the future with confidence that comes from faith in a God who works all things together for good.

As a thank-you, I am offering you these e-books for **FREE**:

- *God and Donald Trump*
- *The Harbinger*
- *I Have Walked With the Living God*
- *Dr. Colbert's Healthy Gut Zone*

To get this **FREE** gift, please go to:

SteveStrangBooks.com/FREE

God bless,